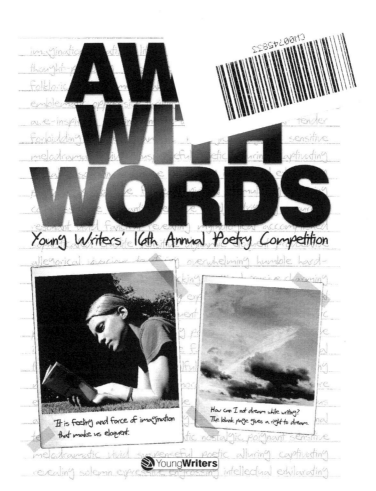

ALL WITH WORDS

Young Writers' 16th Annual Poetry Competition

It is feeling and force of imagination that make us eloquent.

How can I not dream while writing? The blank page gives a right to dream.

YoungWriters

London & The Home Counties
Edited by Mark Richardson

First published in Great Britain in 2007 by:
Young Writers
Remus House
Coltsfoot Drive
Peterborough
PE2 9JX
Telephone: 01733 890066
Website: www.youngwriters.co.uk

SB ISBN 978-1 84431 156 9

Foreword

This year, the Young Writers' *Away With Words* competition proudly presents a showcase of the best poetic talent selected from thousands of up-and-coming writers nationwide.

Young Writers was established in 1991 to promote the reading and writing of poetry within schools and to the young of today. Our books nurture and inspire confidence in the ability of young writers and provide a snapshot of poems written in schools and at home by budding poets of the future.

The thought, effort, imagination and hard work put into each poem impressed us all and the task of selecting poems was a difficult but nevertheless enjoyable experience.

We hope you are as pleased as we are with the final selection and that you and your family continue to be entertained with *Away With Words London & The Home Counties* for many years to come.

Contents

Queens College, London

Ranelagh School, Bracknell

Reading Girls' School, Reading

St Dunstan's College, Catford

St James' Catholic High School, Colindale

St Joseph's Academy, Blackheath

Gus Allman (12)	69
Jesse Kamau (12)	70
Aaron Staff (12)	70
Valence Festus (12)	71
Mohamed Kallon (12)	72
Adrian Masola (11)	73

St Nicholas School, Southend-on-Sea
Jade Reader	73

St Paul's Academy, Plumstead
Heather Ragoonanan (11)	74
Justina Ayowunmi Adu (15)	74
Joseph Stevens (12)	75
Oliver Scorer (12)	75
Jerin Andrews (13)	76
Tamara Carby (11)	76
Nhien Le (12)	77
Rebecca Lee (11)	77
Monika Kersnauskaite (13)	78
Ese Ojo (13)	78
Fiona Arkins (13)	79

St Paul's Girls' School, London
Elizabeth Walker (11)	79
Kaarina Aho (11)	80
Anna Thomas (12)	80
Bethany Aitman (15)	81
Catherine Olver (13)	81
Addy Young (12)	82

Sarah Bonnell School, Stratford
Maria Raji (13)	83
Sophina Mahmood (13)	84
Gulshan Zahra (13)	84
Isabella Ismay (12)	85
Sarah Vincent (13)	85
Ayesha Khanom (12)	86
Ella Becket (13)	86

Nadia Mumtaz Khan (15)   87
Rezwana Akhter (13)   87
Waseema Ahmed (13)   88
Yasmin Ahmed (13)   89
Zara Khan (13)   90

Sir Charles Lucas Arts College, Colchester
Sophie Davies (12)   90
Stephanie Nicholls (12)   91
Coleen Armstrong (13)   92
Cherie Lovage (15)   93
Melissa Walker (15)   94
Michael Johnston (16)   95
Samuel Lees (15)   96

Tendring Technology & Sixth Form College, Clacton-on-Sea
Jade Duller (13)   97
Charlotte Luxford (14)   98
Sam Jones (14)   99
Jessica Webster (14)   100
Terri-Leigh Waters (13)   101
Claire Hills (13)   102
Daniel Wall (13)   103

The Compton School, London
Atlanta Knight (11)   103
Cheryn Jordon (10)   104
Radha Bhatt (12)   105
Lyuben Vachkov (12)   106
Kareem Marsh-Henry (11)   106
Gabriel Akamo (12)   107
Jordan-Louise Day (11)   107
Charlotte Copeland (16)   108
Linda Epstein (11)   109
Tom Heritage (16)   110
Emma Goldsmith (12)   111
Harlan Kohll (13)   112
Anthony Sturt (14)   113
Sh'kyra Jordon (11)   114
Hayley Mansfield (13)   115

The Emmbrook Secondary School, Wokingham

Trevor Roberts School, London

Wellington College, Crowthorne

The Poems

Don't Know The Name

As we close our eyes
And fall to sleep
Zebras flying
Unicorns laughing
As we take a quick peep.

At the world in our minds
The land slumber can release
Shimmering waters
Dancing lights
No hate, just perfect peace.

And I stand on clouds
Drifting in midnight blue,
Head full of lightning,
Hands full of magic,
Singing and swirling for you.

In enchanted forests
Buried in golden tides
No pain
No bitterness
We sit silently side by side.

By day we fit the mould
Ignore remarks that are vicious
But now we're free
Now we fly
Cold hearts can't touch us.

It's only a fantasy
Only in dreams
No pain
No bitterness
In reality
Are ludicrous, it seems.

Michelle Huxter (17)

Beat The Bully

I used to,
Walk around,
Didn't know what to do,
I was lost, but now I'm found.

I'm the one you used to tease,
You called me names for your games,
I was the one begging on my knees,
Hiding my face in shame.

You used to hurt me,
You used to tease me,
I was your broken toy,
You didn't need any tool.
You used to hurt me,
You used to tease me,
I didn't object because I thought you were cool.

I used to,
Cry, cry and cry,
But now I know what to do,
Hold my head up high, high and high.

You won't bully me anymore,
I am recovered from where you hurt me before.
That was when I was shy and small.
But even if I don't look it I now stand up tall.

You used to hurt me,
You used to tease me,
I was your broken toy,
You didn't need any tool,
You used to hurt me,
You used to tease me,
I didn't object because I thought you were cool.

And after all the pain is gone,
I am left with a tear,
It drops from the eye,
Then I sigh,
It's over I am safe here.

But am I?
I ask myself,
Can the horror still get in?
I suddenly feel as small as an elf,
It's as easy as lifting a lid off a tin.

Really no, it cannot be,
Have I really stopped it fully?
Am I really finally free?
Did I really beat the bully?

Shannen Turner (12)

A Case Of Murder

I knew it was a bad idea leaving him alone,
Alone that is except for me.
Why he was only nine
Why couldn't Dad see
What a horrible end for me.
I was sitting all alone in my sleep,
When all of a sudden a pain made me weep.
I woke up to see him staring at me,
Staring at me with an eye full of glee.
I ran and I ran
To find a hiding place
That's when the fight began,
I hissed as I ran,
As fast as I could to a place under the couch.
Under the couch was musty
Not only that it was dusty,
He swung at me again
That was when I knew when
To make a dart for the door,
He hurt me once more
As I landed in a heap on the floor,
He feared I was dead,
With a head full of regret
He scooped me up from the floor,
With a spade, nothing more
And ran with me down the stairs
And left me in a cupboard there,
And cried tears of prayer,
As he wished he'd left me be.
Now when Dad returns
What will he see
For sure not me
The little boy cried
Until he cried his eyes dry,
And headed to the kitchen
To see what he had there.

A rope with a loop
His shoulders dropped,
As he tied the rope to the floor,
Now when Dad returns
His heart will burn
As his family is no more.

Lauren Webb (13)

My Life

I wake up Monday morning,
Oh no it's six o'clock!
I've got to put on my uniform,
And my horrible woollen socks!

I go downstairs to breakfast,
And on the table I see,
A horrible bowl of oatmeal,
And a tasteless cup of tea.

I'm rushing around,
I'm going to be late.
But I'm still in pyjamas,
And my hair is a state!

I get to school eventually,
Twenty minutes behind.
I went to see my teacher,
And the detention slip was signed.

My first two lessons are normal,
Well as normal as they get.
I didn't finish my class work,
And I had loads of homework set.

Next of course was geography,
And after that was maths.
We were doing long division,
I mean, come on, how boring's that!

Afterwards was lunchtime,
And I'd forgotten my lunch.
I asked a girl for a little of hers,
And nearly got a punch!

After lunch was Latin,
That's alright I guess,
But I can safely say with all my heart,
The teacher I do detest.

Next was dreaded detention,
The most boring word I know.
Sometimes I hallucinate,
And think in spring it'll snow.

When I got home,
It wasn't much better,
My mum was quite angry,
She'd got the letter.

You said you left in pyjamas,
Your lying hurts my head,
And then I said in a surrendering voice,
That's it I'm going to bed!

Lauren McDonagh (12)

The Enchanted Garden

I really hate my garden,
It's as boring as can be.
There's nothing good about it,
There's nothing good to see.

There is a mysterious gate,
Right at the very bottom.
But no one ever goes near it,
It's as though it has been forgotten.

Overcome by curiosity,
I decide to take a peek.
I push it slowly with caution,
And it opens with a creak.

A wondrous sight beholds me,
Before my very eyes.
There is an enchanted garden,
Which fills me with surprise.

An array of splendorous colour,
Fairies dancing with delight,
Leprechauns singing joyfully,
Such a glorious sight.

Then I see before me,
The most amazing of things,
A dazzling white unicorn,
With elegant, feathery wings.

It flies towards me gently,
And lands beside the sea.
It sweetly gestures 'climb aboard'
We glide off, him and me.

Soaring high above the clouds,
Things aplenty we can see.
Just the two of us together,
I have never felt such glee.

We land beside a castle,
A princess I am it seems.
Or am I just tucked up in bed,
Lost in my imaginary dreams!

Amelia Allen (12)

The Christmas Angel

It's almost ready,
My grand tree,
Some baubles are the same,
But only one of me.

My curls are still bouncy,
My dress, as always grand,
My wings coated in glitter,
For when I come to land.

The colours of Christmas,
Red, gold and green,
So many decorations, so little space,
All my favourite ornaments hanging
On garlands of satin and lace.

The baubles all different,
Some curvy, fat and round,
Some tall, pointed and twisted,
Classic hymns fill the air
With sound.

Big stockings filled with gifts,
Games, books, all kinds of toys,
Pink paper for the girls,
Blue for the boys.

I will see his bright red sleigh
Owned by the generous old Santa,
With reindeer Rudolph and Dancer,
On the roof, I hear them softly canter.

At last the girl holds me,
And fiddles with my delicate hair,
For without me,
The tree is really quite bare.

I've been picked up,
I hold on tight,
Half-filled with happiness,
Half with fright.

The family stand back
In aghast,
At the magical tree
I'm at the top at last.

Olivia Milne (12)

Morning Routines

Push back the covers,
Walk down the stairs,
Eat up my breakfast,
(Two little pears!)

Up to my bedroom,
Tidy it up,
Put my things away,
Take down an old cup!

Now to the bathroom,
To get myself clean,
Brush my teeth, use the flannel,
Try hard to look keen!

Back to the bedroom,
To get on my clothes,
Smarten up my uniform,
From my head to my toes!

A knock on the door,
I wonder who's there,
It could be a goblin,
Some ghosties *beware!*

I open the door,
As slow as can be,
But when I take a look,
It's just my friend Becky!

I put on my shoes,
I collect my bus fare,
Before I go out though,
I must do my hair!

We run to the bus stop looking like fools,
But finally we get here to *King John School!*

Eloise Taylor (13)

The Future

Robots used in hospitals and war
Trying to save the rich and the poor

Computer chips worn in the ear
To translate and understand foreign languages for you to hear

A solution to reducing the pollution is to
Take a hike, ride a bike or let the electric bus, train or plane
Take the strain

The future for us children is bright
If we respect other cultures, religion and unite
We can choose to learn all we can
Grow up to be an intelligent woman or man
And take care of the world the best way we can.

Levi Tate (12)
Chafford Hundred Campus, Grays

Love Washing Away

I left my love life on the ground
Waiting for the rain to wash me away
But sun is just shining on my love life
Just waiting for it to rain
Finally the rain has washed me away
From my love life.

Andrew Curtis (13)
Chafford Hundred Campus, Grays

Defeat

You can't see me,
Not if you tried,
Because my soul is beyond the eye,
Beauty is skin deep,
Or so they say,
My memories are an exposé,
But where is my heart and where does it lie,
I do not know,
I don't know why,
My heart is ice,
My heart is dead,
As I sleep in my lonely bed,
But you don't know,
You don't know why,
Why every night in pain I cry,
So get out,
And don't come back,
You have broken me,
And now I've cracked,
So goodbye
And goodnight
I'm giving up without a fight.

Louise Bell (14)
Chafford Hundred Campus, Grays

Seconds Before Death

I'm famous and rich, many eyes on me,
I'll be dead soon you shall see.
A bullet in my chest,
You know the rest.
If only I could show my powerful love,
My life spilling out of me,
Similar to a silent dove,
Flying high from up above.

Javan Francis (14)
Chafford Hundred Campus, Grays

Love Is A Dime

Love is like a lump of gold,
It's hard to find and hard to hold,
Love will blossom like a flower,
It takes time not just an hour,
Love is like a hidden treasure,
Once you have found it, it brings such pleasure,
Love gives you the greatest feeling,
And that is why it's so appealing,
Love is like a fragile urn,
Once you've broken it, it won't return,
Love is for everyone, sometimes more than once,
If you get rejected you feel like a dunce,
Love is like a game of Russian Roulette,
You take a chance and see what you get,
Love will blossom over time,
Take it slow,
Love is a dime.

Sam Bennett (14)
Chafford Hundred Campus, Grays

Untitled

Dear Mr Shakespeare, this to you

Why do we have to learn about you?
You don't know what you put us through.

When we read your wild and wacky plays
We are always miserable for days.

Prospero's nutter who lives for magic
Romeo and Juliet is far too tragic.

Your sonnets are hard and not about love
To tell you the truth I think they should
Give you the shove!

Sam Slaney (13)
Chafford Hundred Campus, Grays

My Greatest Memory

I looked up to see,
People clapping and cheering me.
I'd done it - I'd qualified,
I was on my way to Coventry.

Another challenge, another swim,
Another pool to try.
My best strokes - back and breast,
Definitely not fly!

A 50 metre pool,
I had to do my best.
I was in a national gala,
Up against all the rest.

Focus, be strong,
The pool seemed so long,
My family were there to cheer,
But while I was in the water, I couldn't hear.

Heart beating, limbs moving,
Through the water I swam.
I did it, a medal win,
As I stood proud, this is who I am.

Competing in the ISA,
For me will always be,
My greatest memory,
A medal haul,
In a 50 metre pool,
For my proud family to see.

Daniel Cooper (12)
Gosfield School, Halstead

Inside My Eyes

I woke up
Got dressed
Cleaned my teeth
Got the bus to school
As soon as I got there they were chanting

'You're fat, you're fat
Urrr, what are you wearing?
Urrr, look at your hair.'

Well, welcome to my world
Got my books out
Got my pencil case out
Sat down
As soon as I done that they started to chant

'You're fat, you're fat
Urrr, what are you wearing?
Urrr, look at your hair.'

Well welcome to my world.

Went in for lunch
Sat down
Ate my lunch
Walked outside.

They were there all in a big circle chanting

'You're fat, you're fat
Urrr, what are you wearing?
Urrr, look at your hair.'

James Wheeler (13)
Gosfield School, Halstead

I Wish I Could Have My Say

I always like a good walk in the park, it gives me
Memories of the days I had with Clarke.
He was always there with all his support and care.
We always had a pear when we were walking and
Listening to the air.

He was always there when I got bullied,
They always pick on me.
Kicked me.
And get their dog to lick me.
They would hold me down,
And I would just frown
When they called me Crown;
My teeth were gold.
I would just sit there even when I was really cold.

I wish I could be them for one day,
To show them what it's like to be like clay,
For them just to play.
Oh I wish I could have my say.

Luke Jackson (12)
Gosfield School, Halstead

In Her Eyes

It's so scary at night
But I have to be wary
If he comes home tonight,
And wants to start a fight!
I'm not strong enough to fight back
So I just stand while he scratches and hits me.

I was thinking . . .
That if I leave it will make things worse.
He might think of some silly curse.
The kids scream and plea,
For him to stop hitting me!

Deia Sakal (13)
Gosfield School, Halstead

Why Are We Here?

I will tell you the meaning of life
I think it's pleasurable with many down sides
Good careers are one thing, but at least aim for something
Everyone must fulfil their destiny, whatever it is!

Careers lead to money, which leads to cash, which leads
                                                    to awesome
I think having a family is also special, it's good to love and care
                                                    for people

God meant for all of us to shine, as children do
There isn't any of us and them, we're all the same no matter what.

There's still an old saying, which I'm going to tell you

Eat drink and be married!

Ross Collings (13)
Gosfield School, Halstead

In Africa

I sit at home in this cold little hut,
It looks grey and dreary,
. . . and extremely boring.

I am starving,
I look across the road at just desert and dirt
No food there.

My clothes are old,
Messy and ragged,
Maybe I will buy some new ones soon.

No, I can't, I have no money,
What shall I do?
I think I will just sit here and look at the moon.

Lucy Bloodworth (12)
Gosfield School, Halstead

The Third World

One year, one day, one beautiful day,
A man was mowing a field,
Mowing a field of fresh crop,
Lushes o' lushes fresh crop.
He mowed all morning,
He mowed after noon.
Then he thought of poor families
Mourning,
In Africa, India and parts of Asia too.
Not a lot of food to eat,
No fresh water to drink,
And no warm bed to sleep in.
They walk down muddy paths,
Muddy paths full of sewage,
Sewage chucked from their own windows.
If he were to turn back time,
Turn back time to the beginning,
Turn back time to the beginning of poverty,
He would stop it permanently.

William Rimell (13)
Gosfield School, Halstead

If I Could Turn Back Time!

If I could turn back time,
I would be somewhere else,
Where I loved,
And then it would not be so awkward,
Somewhere it felt more like home to me,
And things were happier,
People were happier
Things are OK, but are not the same,
Until we go back,
And pack our stuff in a sack.

Ashleigh Kent (12)
Gosfield School, Halstead

Good Times, Great Memories

Although I don't have many great memories,
I do have one that's better than all the rest.
The day I made my football debut,
When the crowds would cheer and roar.
I played with all my might,
I tackled and slid, passed and set up the striker.
At the end of the game when we had won,
I shouted and cheered.
Shook hands with the opposition,
And finally we went home.

My second memory is of a time with my best mate,
He was called Dennis.
He wasn't that bright but he was still the best,
He helped cheer me up when I was blue.
Every time we went outside we got filthy and wet,
But we always kept coming in the house with a bit of a sweat.
We had a drink and something to eat,
Then we walked to my dad's farm park.
There were sheep, cows and pigs,
With a hoot and a howl they would soon bound away,
So that is two of my happiest memories I've got to stay with me.

Charlie Philip (13)
Gosfield School, Halstead

The Meaning Of Life

Well we are here, to eat, drink, sleep,
The wonders of this is pizza, booze and a waterbed
And watching the big game live
Why bother finding out
Just sit back in your leather recliner
And have a sip of beer.

Jack Partridge (14)
Gosfield School, Halstead

I Didn't Do It!

You have to believe me
I didn't do it
Mum, Dad, please help
I don't want to be here all my life.

It's a scary place in here
I don't want to stay
They think I killed him
But I swear I didn't.

I was in the bar one night
A man walked in
He'd had a bit too much to drink
He started to cause some trouble.

I left the bar late in the night
Then I got a phone call
The bloke had been killed, stabbed in the heart,
So I went back to see for myself.

When I got there the police showed up
They were treating me like a suspect
I knew they thought I did it
They shoved me in the back of the car,
I knew what was going to happen.

So here I am today
Being accused for murder
I don't know if I'm going to get out
So it's bye for now
I didn't do it!

Danny McLintock (14)
Gosfield School, Halstead

Voice Of The Teen

No voice, no ideas, don't know what I want,
Well I do, I may be a teen, but I'm as useful as you,
Hear me, see me, listen to me, acknowledge me,
Speak out like me, stand up like me, be seen like me.

Make a say, change the world, be heard,
Make them give you a word,
You may be young, but yet your life has begun,
Valuable as a gem, yet you're as useful as them.

James Rolfe (14)
Gosfield School, Halstead

Wearing A Simple Hat

How calm can it be the clear blue sky?
I've lost my pen.
The clear blue sky that your eyes can see
The special one with the unique engraved figures
See the simple hat, you set in place with delicate fingers
I can't write without it, it's my imagination
Fingers which shake as the dawn lingers.

It cost me so much, and I borrowed some money
Lingers - the jewels - on the grass in the mist
It's not in my pencil case, it's not in my bag
The mist of the silence concealed in the hush
I promised I'd look after it, this was my last chance.

In the hush you feel courage at the slightest peak
Not under here, or over there . . .

The slightest peak of the sun for darkness to seek
Come on! Where has it gone? Who took it?
Seek light to turn silver as the glittering moon
Oh, behind my ear all along.

Sanjidah Sabur (13)
Queens College, London

Anger

My anger rises, my fists clench
My knees bend, my whole body stiffens.
That's when it happens,
I collapse onto my bed in tears
And squeeze my teddy like a child . . .

I know I lost it, my cool I mean.
I wish that you could understand
Life in my shoes, in my head too.
I wish we could cross the bridge to each other's hearts
But we are too scared we'll fall.

I know, I know the consequences, I say,
That's when anger comes back
Like a punch in the stomach.
If only you could understand,
But I can't explain things in your language.

Sacha Werbeloff (12)
Queens College, London

Freedom

I have a lust for freedom
I know that one day I will have freedom
But for now freedom is for dreaming
While I am sleeping.
Freedom is the rainbow.
Freedom is the sun.
Freedom is the moon.
And one day I will be one with freedom.
My passion for freedom is soft like a velvet pearl,
But fighting for freedom is hard like a rock.
If I could break through that rock,
This could be the start of something new.

Clemmie Hastings (14)
Queens College, London

Success

I'm on the starting line at last,
If I'm going to be an athlete I must win.
Jingle Bells - that tune, rings in my head,
I will win, I will win.
I'd hate to disappoint my mum and dad -
I'd hate to leave here in disgrace . . .

It's time to focus now, make it a long and easy race:
The prize is *gold,* not silver like the moon.
Listen to the crowd, they're cheering wildly,
And all for me, you'll see, you'll see!
I will win, I will win, I'm going to win . . .

My enemy's moved closer,
He's as jealous as can be,
He's throwing pebbles at my shoes,
I stoop and stumble, let him catch me up,
Until the crowd's incredible cheers pull
My hopes back to me.

I regain my confidence, as the cheat is taken out,
Soon I'll win the money, and buy a house or holiday,
Because the prize is meant for me.
I will win, I will win, I'm going to win.
I have to have that money,
I run like the wind,
Like a dog chasing a hare.

Tiredness is dragging me down,
Like sand sinking into water,
But it is over now, and I have won . . .

Darya Khaneghah (13)
Queens College, London

Vortex

Regret's eating me, inside to out.

I can't run, I can't hide,
Regret is coming, it's coming for me.

Regret is a demon sucking the life from me,
Each move,
Each step is so hard to take.

Regret feeds on irresponsibility.
On my 'not caring' what to do,
On my 'not thinking' before I speak,
Or what will happen before I do it . . . count to ten.

Regret is something I can't ignore.
I have everything; yet my world feels so incomplete,
I have family, yet they don't know me,
I have friends, but I don't know them,
I have a house, but I don't own it . . .

Regret is overpowering me,
It fills each day with thought and dreams that you can't understand.
I can't run, I can't hide,
It's no use trying, it's coming for me -
I know it's arrived;
Life is a meaningless vortex . . .

Annoushka Reger-Claremont (12)
Queens College, London

The Wishing Tree

I ran to my tree, my Wishing Tree
And sobbed for Tiger our cat
Squashed under the wheels of a car.

What will Mum and Ivan say?
It's all my fault, I should have watched
I can't tell the truth, but I can't lie
So I haven't told anyone yet -
Will they hate me if I do?

Guilt is swelling up in me,
It wants to spurt, but I won't let it,
I'm afraid of what I'll say.

I cried myself to sleep that night
And I dreamed and I dreamed;

Of a cat with wings
Of a cat with wings that spoke to me:

>It was fluffy and pink and white,
>And it climbed my tree
>And picked the fruit.

>It was magical, young,
>It was shy and naïve,
>And it brought me the kernels of truth
>To share with my family.

Jaime Shuttleworth (13)
Queens College, London

Happiness

Darya, enveloped in her black dress,
Sat alone in the bare bedroom remembering
Her mother's words, 'Happiness catches you when you least
Expect it, like the news popping from the page.'

The thought cheered her for a moment,
But loneliness and the feeling of being
So unwanted, cut off from the rest of the world,
Like flood water, surrounding everything and everyone.

'Think cheerful,' mother said, 'think of trickling water,
The soft song of children, the taste of lemon-lime lollies,
Home-made cakes, cookies - happiness comes like
The smell of summer and goes like the wind swirling
The mass of leaves.'

And so Darya put on a white dress,
With yellow flowers - a dress to change
The cycle of never-ending unhappiness -

And she went down to the warm colourful garden
Where children were singing
And licking lemon lollies and there she stayed
Suddenly bathed in a wash of her own happiness.

Celia Hart (13)
Queens College, London

Human Or Animal?

I am captured in an area where an animal acts as if he has had
No attention,
Where he sulks,
Where he has his back towards me.

But when I am up and standing,
It's as if he's a new person.
A human trapped in a dog's body.

I feel the vibes of energy coming towards me,
His excitement,
His tail spins around like a helicopter.

And as he knocks into me,
Giving me a huge heartwarming hug,
I am feeling the thickness of his fur,
And his paws too big for his body, trampling on my feet
Like a heavyweight.

And then there is the question.
What is he?
Is he a human trapped in a dog's body?

Anouska Cave (12)
Queens College, London

Evening

And the no-face girl
sits on the slate roof.

Believing that everything is her fault,
that everyone is blaming her, for
what happened, after the party . . .

The no-face girl
is afraid that everyone has seen
the real her, the face behind the mask.
She wishes she could put the clocks back,
put the armour on, but no, everything went wrong.

The no-face girl
is sitting, choking back the acidic taste
of regret. The cool twilight breeze
rustling through her hair,
tells the tale of her sinful past.

On the roof,
listening to the buzzing bees
whispering to each other.

The no-face girl feels
filthy worms squirming around
her head. She grasps her knees,
hold onto your sanity . . .

She thinks fast,
breathe, keep breathing -

> *Don't lose your nerve.*
> *The king's men are coming*
> *to put Humpty Dumpty together again.*

Bella Saltiel (13)
Queens College, London

The Rackatoof

His legs tangled one another,
Into one big knot.
His long swift tail swept up into the air,
Passing a breeze to his face.
His eyelashes curled over his diamond eyes,
I could see he was smiling,
When I looked into his eyes,
But when I looked down at his red, wet lips,
I could still smell, hear, see
And feel that smile,
That same smile that wasn't there,
I stepped back and stared at him
But something was missing,
Something didn't fit,
As if his face was a jigsaw
And there was a missing piece
And then it struck me
Like a jolt of lightning
Running through my veins,
It was the frown that didn't fit
With the diamond eyes,
The elegant twining legs
The red rosy cheeks
That almost looked as if
They had been painted on with a
Soft, red, wet paintbrush
But the frown almost looked as if it
Had been painted on with a rough,
Old grey paintbrush.
His legs untangled one another
From that one big knot.

Darcey Wise (12)
Queens College, London

Jealousy

The whistle's blown, the race is on,
I'm running hard, I'm going to win.
I'm trying my hardest,
But she's picking up speed,
A short gust of wind goes past; I think she is overtaking me.

My chameleon eyes turn green,
As green as the monster inside of me.
She doesn't deserve the prize, I do,
Miriam, Miriam, miraculous Miriam
She doesn't deserve the prize, I do.

My throat is clogged with jealousy,
I want the prize; I want to win -
Hatred stales my tongue,
I hear it roaring in my head,
She doesn't deserve the prize, I do.

Tatiana Sieff (13)
Queens College, London

Fantasy Poem

He gallops through the woods, engraving the surface of the ground
His sleek figure, standing tall in the fiery light.
The peace around him echoes like laughter,
He reaches down, four hands touch.

I touch his back; it's smooth and soft like suede.
He stares at me, his eyes scorching yellow.
I watch him, as his ears prick up.
He listens to the sound;
The river, the wind, the birds, the trees.
Silence!
He smiles.

Isabelle Josephs (13)
Queens College, London

The Fliteroge

He speeds across the meadows bright,
Orange and yellow blurs
The Fliteroge had never been seen
The rare agile creature.

His large crystal eyes shine when hit by sun
A vortex of emerald reflections,
Bouncing into rays of light
Endless brightness.

Alone in the Earth, no one to talk to
It flutters around all by itself,
No companions
So no one knows the truth
Is he a myth or reality?

Atalandi Dixon (12)
Queens College, London

The Fox

The cinnamon-coated fox,
As still as the mountain rocks,
As soundless as pure quiet,
Instead of a great riot.
His eyes squinting with fear,
His prey is near.
Breath crisp and bold,
From the sparkling cold.
The silence all around,
He can hear the smallest sound.
What a shame it's ending,
While the gunshots are mending.

Sarah Melina Al-Sowaidan (13)
Queens College, London

Fantasy

It lives alone
Sleeping where the rainbows end,
I saw it once,
When walking round a bend.

It sings a tune
As it prances,
It is a rare sight
You don't get many chances
To see it drinking from a lake
Of pure gold,
Its tune is soft and delicate
Yet still proud and bold.

The moon's liquid glow
Is another tasty meal,
It also helps the wind blow
I wish I had seen it more than once.

It shows the sun where to shine
It tells the sun tricks like;
Your rays don't have to be in a straight line.

I know I'll find it one day again
But for now
I'll have to stay on the bay
And dream of hearing that touching tune
Once again.

Mariette Moor (13)
Queens College, London

The Fire Bird

A creature you have never seen,
Just stepped into my house.
A bird that has never been,
In a human's home.

A bird that you might think
An owl or a swan,
And you are scared to blink,
Afraid it might be gone.

Then the bird comes closer,
Its multicoloured eyes
Are filled with wisdom, knowing,
Its burning feathers glowing.

The bird opened its wings,
Its golden, red and orange wings,
As if it's to embrace you
Or show it trusted you.

The burning red tail
Swished from side to side,
Just like a dog when happy,
Or nervous, worried waiting.

It just came closer,
Looks into your eyes,
Hopes you understand
That this is not a lie.

Zhaniya Alshinbayeva (12)
Queens College, London

Have You Ever . . . ?

Have you ever looked at the end of the garden?
Where the forests of weeds start to grow
Have you ever looked under the mushrooms?
To see what is lurking under its shadow.

Have you ever seen a fairy?
The flower petal dresses or their silk faces
Have you ever seen a pixie?
Its mischievous dance or its cheeky grin.

Have you ever seen a fairy's note?
The tiny writing or the perfect ink
Have you ever heard of the pixie's music?
Quiet and loud or soft and staccato.

Have you ever, had you ever?
Have you ever heard a baby cry?
Have you ever, had you ever?
Seen a fairy or pixie fly by . . . ?

Emily Crowder (13)
Queens College, London

Fast But Slow

The creature moved so slowly,
With its long skinny legs, with its bailey coat,
And lavender swirl.
The misty green reflected from its dirty eyes,
A proud look came in its expressionless face,
It was like; I didn't deserve to be near him.

He turned gracefully,
With his head held high,
Looked over his shoulder,
And happened to pass by.
With the tread of leaves,
Squashing beneath his feet,
He disappeared as quickly as he had come.

Lydia Bowden (13)
Queens College, London

The Fairy

So elegant, so delicate,
Emerald eyes shine like jewels,
Golden hair, a silky waterfall flowing down her back.

Pale skin, as soft as velvet,
Sweeping over the leaves,
Quiet as a mouse.

The fairy, dancing through the flowers,
Fluttering in the breeze,
Tiny feet touching the cool water of the lake.

Fairies all across the forest,
Incandescent in the moonlight,
Diamonds dripping from their fingers.

Watching autumn unfold,
A world of wonder,
So elegant, so delicate.

Maud Einhorn (12)
Queens College, London

Sanctuary

Hostility hangs in the air,
Loneliness lingers just to remind you,
Memories flash 'cross their love-hungry faces,
Dreaming of when they had homes not just places.

Innocence shines off neglected young,
Sad, hopeless pride shows in the elderly,
Wishful but doubtful expressions on all,
Eager to hear their new owners call.

Happiness starts to spark,
Recognition to flow,
Solitude diminished,
All misery finished.

Elizabeth Morgan (11)
Ranelagh School, Bracknell

Here Comes The Rain!

Clouds, clouds everywhere,
Darkening by the minute,
Heaving with heavy raindrops,
Desperate to get out,
'Roar' cries the clouds,
Here comes the rain,
Pitter-patter on the roof,
Heading straight for *me*.

Whispering to each other,
Whispering everywhere,
Drip drop here and there,
Falling on my hair.

But now the rain has stopped, a rainbow
Has appeared, the raindrops
Have all popped, and a smile
Is now here!

Victoria Harding (12)
Ranelagh School, Bracknell

The Kraken

In the deep of the sea's embrace,
It maims and hates the human race.
Dragging ships from the light,
Always futile is the fight.

In the gloomy water lurks,
A giant beast that nothing hurts.
Destroying all in its path,
Lo and behold its dreaded wrath.

Back to its cave it does plunge,
Surrounded by enormous sponge.
Ruling over the seaweed bracken,
All men beware: The Kraken!

Lyndon Nossell & Patrick Munro (12)
Ranelagh School, Bracknell

Rugby

I was runnin' up and down the pitch
Lookin' for the ball.
I stopped and looked and there it was
Popping out the maul.
A man in blue screamed, 'Down on it!'
He looked quite fierce and cruel.

It rolled away in front of me,
I jumped right on the ball.
A pile of meat, a sweaty heat,
Ran at me like a fool.
Stand up, I say, stand up to him,
Out of this muddy pool.

The impact was so very hard
Knocked me into the air.
I roared with pain and screamed again,
As I had no arm to spare.
Got carried off in agony, blood dripping from my hair,
From the pitch into a room where they would give me care.

Samuel Swanborough (13)
Ranelagh School, Bracknell

How Can That Be My Mother?

(Inspired by Pam Ayres)

How can that be my mother? How can she be so nice?
She always used to shout at me. Now she's thinking twice.

How can that be my mother? Her fashion sense is mad.
Through all the years of looking good, she now looks really bad.

How can that be my mother? I really want to shout.
Her long blonde locks are missing, her hair has fallen out.

How can that be my mother? Asleep in that chair.
She used to be so active, now she's hardly there.

Abbie Perrins (12)
Ranelagh School, Bracknell

That Special Book

When you open
That special book,
There's a whole new world,
For you to look.

A city, time has forgot,
Sunk way, way undersea
A desert world,
Unlocked by key.

A sweltering jungle,
Full of bug and beast,
An ancient castle,
With a lavish feast.

But when you finish,
The adventure halts,
You're back, the real world,
With all your silly faults.

Emily Peach (12)
Ranelagh School, Bracknell

Springer Spaniel

Springer Spaniels are full of fun,
So lively, always on the run,
Bred for catching game for the gun.

Brown floppy ears framing their face,
Powerful legs giving them pace,
Creatures hide in fear of a chase.

By nature loving and loyal,
They look incredibly royal,
So very hard not to spoil.

Liam Gallagher (13)
Ranelagh School, Bracknell

My Embarrassing Mother -
How Can That Be My Mother?

(Inspired by Pam Ayres)

How can that be my mother?
What happened to her hair?
Since when was it that ugly,
To make people stop and stare?

How can that be my mother?
How can she dress like that?
She used to have good dress sense,
But now she just looks fat!

How can that be my mother?
Why does she make such a fuss?
She treats me like a little kid,
But I'd rather catch the bus!

How can that be my mother?
Why does she embarrass me so?
She always tries to fit in,
But really, she should go!

Cati Vacher (12)
Ranelagh School, Bracknell

Shipwreck

S ilent ship with the ghosts that stalk
H ide, they do, from the divers who walk
I t screams but no one hears
P irates killed the people over the years
W hen fish aren't looking and they are gone
R evolting pirates swim on and on
E very single ship is scary
C onquered like the ship named Mary
K iller creatures lurk about; you shouldn't go there
   It's not a doubt.

Sophie Hammond (12)
Ranelagh School, Bracknell

Nature's Secret

Birds and butterflies
All like pies
But that means nothing at all
What's more important is their call.

The call of nature, oh so sweet
Like the soft drum's beat
The tree's knees
Are covered by bees.

The sea tries to wave
All over the cave
And the air like bears
Has claws but no one seems to care.

So that is nature's secret, oh so sweet
Like the parakeet
I like music with a beat
And want to know how nature is so sweet.

Joshua Grant (11)
Ranelagh School, Bracknell

Rumours

Rumours are lies that get out of hand,
First they are small, and then they are grand.
You don't mean to say something, but someone else hears,
And then quickly your friendship is ending in tears.
Rumours are horrible, they don't listen, don't care,
They end all the friendships that are so hard to repair.
You should ignore all the rumours, the lies, the deceit,
Travelling through classmates, they repeat and repeat.
All you want to do is stop them, make people see sense,
All you can do is watch them, hide away in defence.
Rumours are lies; they drive you around the bend,
Rumours are loathsome; they end your friends.

Shannon Thwaites (13)
Ranelagh School, Bracknell

Rain, Rain, Rain

As the rain comes falling down,
Across the rivers, streets and towns.

While it rains I start to think,
Will the world ever sink?

Maybe today, maybe tomorrow,
It will fill the world with lots of sorrow.

Is today the last day I see,
All the rain fall on me.

I look across the sky so high,
Thinking to myself

Wondering when the rain will stop,
Is it possible for the world to overflow
And begin to drop?

Jonathan Tellyn (12)
Ranelagh School, Bracknell

The Prisoner

I'm stuck here all alone.
No one else but me.
I want my family most of all,
To take me home,
To be free.

I'm stuck here all alone,
Only if they knew,
I'm innocent,
I'm sure,
Sitting on this freezing floor.

I'm stuck here all alone,
No food, no water,
Help! Help! I loudly cry,
But no one comes,
I am about to die.

Edward Clapham (12)
Ranelagh School, Bracknell

Can You See The Real Me?

I am a person
Take a look at me
I live in London
The posh side you see.

I really want someone to know me
For who I really am
You'll scream and jump at me
Like I'm not human.

I'm frozen like a picture
When I'm on a bus
I want to shriek,
Shout and make a fuss.

I am a celebrity
A movie star can you see?
Did you know
No of course not . . .

Because no one knows the real me . . .

Jessica Potter (12)
Ranelagh School, Bracknell

Winter To Spring

Just a little while ago,
All the ground was white with snow.
Trees and plants were dry and bare,
Not a sign of life was there.

But now the buds and leaves are seen,
Now the fields are bright and green.
Pretty birds are on the wing,
With a joyful song they sing.

Oh how I love the pleasant spring!

Kayleigh Conway (12)
Ranelagh School, Bracknell

The Market

The earth was as hot
As the sun in the sky,
And all you could hear
Were the vendor's long cries.

The place was crowded
With people all around,
But they didn't seem
To make a sound.

After a while
The crowd died down,
And then it seemed
Like there was no town.

As the day was drawing now
The great big sun took a bow,
The moon took its place in the air
And that was the end of the market fair.

Holly Simpson (11)
Ranelagh School, Bracknell

The Ashes!

The Ashes series came down to this ball,
The final of the test
The English team stood in the field
Hoping for the best
The bowler steamed towards the crease
Where the batsman stood afraid,
The ball, it thundered out his hand,
Left the batsman in a daze
The ball slammed down onto ground, rocketed towards the clouds
It hit the batsmen in the head and the thud was awfully loud
The batsman collapsed on the wickets,
And the fielding team appealed
The umpire put his finger up and the victory was sealed.

Charlie Johnson (11)
Ranelagh School, Bracknell

The Page And The Poet

The paper sat wordless on the table,
Seeing as the poet was clearly unable
To write a letter, word or phrase,
This pen just would not amaze.

The poet needed some inspiration,
But unfortunately, his determination,
Was falling rapidly like a brick,
When suddenly a little kick
Came inside the poet's head
Finally the page was fed.

Little words came bouncing on,
When amazingly the page was gone.
Hidden beneath all the letters
Now the poet felt much better.

Now the page has been mended
Regrettably the poem's ended.

Milly Munday (12)
Ranelagh School, Bracknell

The Cheetah

(Inspired by Tennyson's 'The Eagle')

He scans the plains with his sharp eye
Waiting so patiently he lies
Fixed on his target, gazelle pie.

The dusty earth beneath him cracks
His legs spring load for the attack
There he waits for that tasty snack.

Adam Monkhouse (13)
Ranelagh School, Bracknell

You And Me

If only he knew how much I cared,
And of this love, that needs be shared.
I can't explain just how I feel,
But this love is deep, it's strong, it's real.

I've tried and tried to walk away,
But knowing you're there just makes me stay.
I remember all the times we've shared,
In your arms, I thought you cared.

We're not together, but I still cry,
As my love for you will never die.
We can share our love and share our hate,
I'll keep on smiling, it's never too late.

To you I may be just a girl,
But boy, to me you mean the world.
I look at you and all I see,
Is us together. You and me.

I gave this love all but a doubt,
It's you I cannot live without.
I don't think you know about the pain,
Caused by you, yet again.

So forget the others, forgive the lies,
Forget your first love, and give this one a try.
This game we're playing we can win together,
And I promise I'll love you forever and ever.

Mollie Bylett (13)
Ranelagh School, Bracknell

How Does It Feel?

I sit in the corner alone,

I whimper, I watch
They stare, they laugh

I feel like I'm the only one,
With no one to care.

I'm there, I know
They don't think about what they are doing.

They hurt
I cry
They taunt
I run

They push
I trip

I slowly fade away.

Jessica Street (11)
Ranelagh School, Bracknell

History Paper

Today is today, tomorrow is tomorrow,
But yesterday made history.
History of good, history of bad, history
Of fun, history of sad.
You are history, whatever you do is
History.
But do you know the one mystery behind
History . . . ?

Lara Winter (11)
Ranelagh School, Bracknell

Why?

No one likes me,
What have I done,
Have I done wrong?

Can I put it right,
Or is it irreversible?
Why me?

Is there a key,
To open the door,
To put the past behind me?

In the corner,
No one there,
Just me and my hurt feelings.

Do you know how it feels?
To be bullied,
Well I do. Why?

Charlie Corfield (11)
Ranelagh School, Bracknell

The Spider

(Inspired by Tennyson)

The spider crawls through his big nest,
Where all his past meals rot and rest,
The humans think of him, a pest.

So many people do despise,
To see him with so many eyes,
He hides his cruelty with his size.

Anna Taylor (13) & Emmy Rickett (12)
Ranelagh School, Bracknell

The One

I remember the time when you took my hand,
Led me to a place that was so grand,
Thinking about this memory, no one will know,
The secret inside I should tell.

Looking down at the ground,
Tears roll off my face,
You lift me up with no disgrace,
Make me laugh, make me smile,
With this memory could last more than a while.

Holding you in my arms for ever and always,
Memories die like open doorways,
To open this memory, time will only tell,
When I find my love for you again.

I will reveal to the world,
That you're my man,
You took my hand without a plan,
Feeling so happy and so free,
I knew that you were the one for me.

To this day I will never forget,
The smile on my face when we first met
Young and charming,
Those were the days,
As I remember we were engaged.

Both together hand in hand,
Walking together we look so grand,
To this day I still remember what I said,
This memory I will keep until I am dead.

Neelum Akram (15)
Reading Girls' School, Reading

Our Love

Love.
Love is beautiful, love is surreal,
It is something you do or something you feel.

Love is a blanket of affection and care,
It's one in a million, it's something rare.

Love is like an eagle soaring through the sky,
It makes you feel like all is possible; it makes you feel high.

Love is a connection, a bond between two,
Something that was once shared, by me and you.

There once was a time when we had this connection,
It's true, it was me and you.

I loved you like no other; you were my heart and soul,
To make you happy was my only goal.

But now, you're gone, why do I feel this pain?
Like I'm standing in the cold, in the pouring rain.

I feel numb and drained, tired and empty,
And all I see, is those times and memories.

When it was me and you,
When you told me I was everything to you, it's true.

You told me, forever, we'd be this way,
But you left me, I remember, it was a cold and windy day.

I called you, again and again and again,
But you were gone, forever, since then.

I loved you; I gave you all of me, and you
Betrayed my trust, it's true.

Now there's nothing left, just a memory or two,
Of happiness, of sadness, of me and you.

Saba Hifza Muneer (14)
Reading Girls' School, Reading

Friendship!

Friendship - the sacred bond me and you share,
When I need you you're always there,
And all because you promise to care.

You're always so thoughtful,
And when I'm down you make me hopeful,
So I promise to do the same for you.

It's true, what's mine is yours,
I love you, I really hope it shows,
And want you to know my heart
And soul is always yours.

I'll always remember and cherish you,
And I really hope you feel the
Same way for me too.

What we have is something rare,
Our friendship isn't something to rip or tear,
But something special for us to share.

Asma Muneer (12)
Reading Girls' School, Reading

Where Is The Heaven On Earth?

Looking down from up above,
At first I see all the doves,
Flying so high, flying so free,
They make me smile,
But only for a while.

As I look further down below,
And then suddenly lose the glow!
The things I see make me want to weep and cry,
Are my eyes deceiving me?
Or is the world so mean to thee?

All the homeless, all the clotheless,
And all I can say is, 'God bless.'
All the bombs, all the attacks, all the barbaric fights,
A tear drops out of my eye,
I am disgraced at the pitiful sight.

> I close my eyes,
> And think to myself,
> Where is the:
> *Heaven on Earth?*

Shamma Raza   (15)
Reading Girls' School, Reading

The Reflection

I gaze into a picture;
One of a little girl; all alone,
I am sucked into it; as fluid in a straw.

In a shattered world I stand -
The Earth desiccated and barren;
Smoke clogging my nostrils; my senses.
The sickening resonance of gunfire,
The constant humming of machinery,
The deafening cry of the missiles . . .
Yes, that is the sweet tune they sing.

I remember the days of smiles;
Days of laughter and cries -
Now overflowing with hushed stillness.

I sit in a corner; amidst shadows where shots pass,
My misty ears teary, fatigued;
Perceived too much of human sacrifice.
Have you ever had to extend your hand?
Seize stones to protect your beloved?
If my eyes were yours,
Clearly, you'd shatter.

Yet, I only struggle in defence;
With stones in my hands;
It is perpetual.

As I stare into the picture,
Fear grips my heart; never to let go -
But even in this fear-gripped spirit of mine,
Subsists a guiding glow,
A cocoon of hope
Soon to metamorphose into a vibrant, simmering butterfly
And fly without restrain; without fear.

Tagrid Musarrat (15)
Reading Girls' School, Reading

Revelations By The Window

Weedier than most boys your age,
The Bible is a golden house in your hands.
You could probably sleep inside it.

But: 'Leave-me-alone-I-have-five-minutes-to-finish-this.'

What on earth are you? If you knew that
You'd keep it to yourself, you wouldn't tell.
If you knew that you'd read something else.
It's no day for that, though, surely? For Revelations by the window?

You know books rot, not like bones
Or rugby trophies, weep and curl to dust
Just to mingle with sweat from fifty years' thumbs -
A library-powder that
Leaps with every
Page-flick.
By now you've inhaled a whole desert of it.

You have the word, man's first disobedience, the fruit,
Moses and the Jews stumbling down your veins,
Various disciples, and two of every animal stuck
In a lump down your trachea;
You have Jesus coating the lining of your lungs.

Fuller anyhow than if
You were to let the wind erode you
Or a tonne of rugby limbs thunder down
And engrave your soul in the grass. Today
Has unsculpted itself and you are definitely
Somewhere else now, opened up and blinded by some star
Or another that won't be debated, debased, debarred -

Your hands thick with pages for five minutes
In a sea of dusty echoing palms.

Annie Katchinska (17)
St Dunstan's College, Catford

A Baby's Dummy

A dummy in a puddle!
A murder?
A kidnap?
It doesn't make sense
Let's look a little further
And see what's over the fence.

The baby was there
Over in the spotlight
With curly blonde hair
There one minute, gone the next
Whatever shall we do to find the evidence?

The mother's worried sick
Her baby's gone missing
Is this just a silly trick?

11 million?
7 million?
3 million?
What will be the charge
Next time for this baby to be back in her mother's arms?

It's a wonder to me why someone
Would do such a thing
But was that in the person's mind?
When the baby was snatched
From the scene of the crime?

It's left up to me
I am the key
I am not a police woman
No, I am anonymous
I need to find out why there was that
Dummy in a puddle.

Emma Maguire (12)
St James' Catholic High School, Colindale

What Is School?

School is boring
School is dull
As if I never knew
Where I left my skull.

School is lame
What a very bad name
Mr Present's to blame
That's why he never came!

Where is music?
Where is maths?
What's an A-Z?
And how is art and crafts?

Teachers chewing chewing gum
They're also drinking rum
And now they've lost their noses
They can't smell any roses!

Stand on the left
Die on the right
Ignore the two children
Who are gonna start a fight.

I'm staring at the flower
Thank God it's nearly lunch hour
The teacher's speaking in French
I'm sorry I broke the bench!

I'm staring at the clock
It's talking tick-tock
Is the teacher in detention
Or will she buy a pension?

School's finished, it's half day
I came in March and left in May!

Andrei Balan (11)
St James' Catholic High School, Colindale

My Love For My Mum

My mother, my mother
Who is she you say
Just the most beautiful
Mother in every way
If I placed the top ten
Divas from around the world
They would not compare
Because my mother comes one of a kind
And not to share
If my mother was going to
Get shot with a gun
I would jump in front of the speeding bullet to save my mum
My mother she loves me so that's why I am doing
This to show my appreciation
My mum you beat the lot
My mum you come out on top
My mum congratulations you deserve the praises.

      Well done Mum.

Shaquelle Hendricks (11)
St Joseph's Academy, Blackheath

Starlight

Starlight friend
Who wanted to
Live in
Harmony.

Starlight friend
With a smile of
Happiness
That never burnt
Away.

Starlight friend
Why did you have
To go?

Dekota Navarda (11)
St Joseph's Academy, Blackheath

Day And Life - Good And Evil

Good and evil
Night and day
First one does not exist
Without the second one.

When people are crying
And one in fear
That is evil.

When people are laughing
And playing
That's good.

Birds are singing and the sun is bright
Bright as a sunflower
Bright as yellow paint
That's the day.

If schools are closed and sky is black
Dark as coffee
Dark as a panther
That's the night.

Evil, day, night and good
Darkness or light
There's always one in your heart
Which are you following
You decide . . .

Andrew Fledrzynski (14)
St Joseph's Academy, Blackheath

City Jungle

It's all the same, there are lots of buildings,
Long and tall and before you know it,
You start to feel claustrophobic.
It's all the same, they're long and tall
And before you know it
You're under the spell of the city jungle.

Marcus Stewart (11)
St Joseph's Academy, Blackheath

Love Is . . .

Love is a radiant beauty,
Love is a real cutie,
Love is like a bird,
Flying freely but not in a herd,
Love can never be judged,
But it cares so much,
Love can be anything,
It can be a necklace or a ring,
Love has a sort of shine,
Love is yours, love is mine,
Love makes you happy,
It doesn't make you snappy,
Love is like a flower,
Generating its beauty and power,
But most of all, love can happen to anybody.

Frankie Knight (13)
St Joseph's Academy, Blackheath

Life

When you carry a knife you think you protect your life
You think you're bad
But you're actually sad.

When you're in a gang you think you're the best
But you need a rest
And most of these people end up under arrest.

You have to love God to have a good life
Not to hold a knife
God is the only one
You are his son
A gun is not your mum.

Marlon Pavenello
St Joseph's Academy, Blackheath

My Life Story

Growing up with my mum was a struggle
Do one thing wrong and it will pop her bubble
All my life she grew up sad
Because me and my family grew up without a dad.

No one to tell me how to kick ball
No one to tell me the wrong or right rule
No one to guide me until I got tall
But now I realise I don't need him at all

You see my life has been hard enough
Every day of my life was a bit tough
Secondary school starting to get rough
Kids telling me to do the wrong stuff.

Dylan Barrett (12)
St Joseph's Academy, Blackheath

Following The Wrong Gang

In school I used to be a fool,
Taking matters in my hands and arriving with new tools.
I was known to be the boy, who was too big for my shoes,
Bullying youngers who didn't want to act cool.

The day came when I was gonna graduate,
But the headmaster was blabbing on about how to calculate.
It was a big day for me as I was being watched,
And reviewed on my 'successfully changed behaviour.'

I was finally out of school,
And following my own rule.
I chased the wrong gang,
Now I'm selling fag, ten pounds each and you get a free tag.

Kelvin Adu Darko (12)
St Joseph's Academy, Blackheath

My School Life

Wake up in the morning cold as ice
Knowing that school is warm and nice
I can go to get a bite to eat
Plenty of my friends to meet
Loads of lessons are fun
Knowledge shoots to my head
Like a bullet from a gun
Lunchtime arrives my stomach groaning
The line is so long everyone's moaning
The end of day bell rings
One of my favourite things
So that's another day finished and done
Knowing that tomorrow's a fresh new one.

Corin Clarke (12)
St Joseph's Academy, Blackheath

Night-Time

Afraid to walk alone at night
Scared of people who roam to fight
Hide your money, hide your phone
You feel the need to run straight home
Footsteps swiftly creep up upon you
You close your eyes and wish
You could just wake up
In complete bliss where there would not be a
Care in the world.

Chavez James (14)
St Joseph's Academy, Blackheath

My Face

That car crash made me a wreck,
Now I feel neglected, almost like Shrek,
I was a sweet boy, everyone liked me,
If girls had a crush, they tended to fight me,
I always fitted in, and was never left out,
I had some great looks; I was never in doubt.
I used to always 'cherps' the girls with my 'broke' down phone,
I always had company and was never alone,
All around school, I was known as the 'cool guy'
I was slick and smooth, just like a samurai,
People used to say, I always knew what to do,
But it seemed that night, I didn't have a clue,
I used to laugh and giggle and enjoy life,
I dreamed of a family, kids and wife,
But now that's all vanished, into that night,
When he crashed into that car, it gave me a fright,
Why did I do it, and bring my friend as well?
I'm scared of my face; I want a long veil,
Now every day, I'm scared of the mirror,
There's a hole in my face, and it makes me shiver,
I hate my face; it's a maze of scars,
I solemnly declare, I truly hate cars,
Now I guess it's the end, my life is all over,
My life is drawing in, I'm feeling closure,
I'm so disgusted, my parents despise me,
I guess in the future, I need to choose wisely,
But my face is torn up! My life is torn up!
I'm going too far, I need to shut up.

Gus Allman (12)
St Joseph's Academy, Blackheath

Sounds Of Life

As I wake up I hear the sweet, sweet sounds of the early birds,
As I walk towards my car I hears the sweet, sweet sounds of
Children having fun.
As I turn my car on I hear the sound of the roaring engine of my car.
As I drive I hear, I hear people arguing about simple things in life.
As I drive I hear more bad sounds of people shouting, 'Fight,
Fight, fight, fight.'
So I get out of my car and walk up to them and say, 'A life is
Extremely precious because you'll only get one.'
As I make my way to my car, a sweet little girl comes to me
And says, 'Thank you.'
As I drive, I think about the little sweet girl and why she had said
Thank you to me.

Jesse Kamau (12)
St Joseph's Academy, Blackheath

My Morning

Wake up in the morning
Face still a mess
Get in the shower
'Get out,' says my mum
Bit annoyed so put up the middle finger not the thumb
Go to school, not interested in learning a thing
Pencil, pen, ruler, all the things I have to bring
To be truthful don't want to do a thing
Because it's so boring . . .

Aaron Staff (12)
St Joseph's Academy, Blackheath

Cook

I thought music was my future until I learned how to cook
Influenced by Jamie Oliver, also read all of his books
Left the music industry, went to university,
Took my studies seriously, and got to where I want to be.

Now I'm in the city, running my own restaurant
I cook the best meal, I can't stop getting customers
More money, more problems, exactly what I'm facing
Even my homeboys are getting jealous
And starting to hate me.

Jealousy isn't going to take you further
When it makes you cross the line, the result could be murder.

But that's the life I chose, and the life I'm going to finish
I'm going to continue with my dreams
Instead of letting them vanish.

As soon as I got my first cheque
People have been after me
They have been spying, trying to 'fig' out my recipe.

Because I hid it wisely, they are trying out plan B
But that isn't going to work either, they should think of plan C

You can be what you want to be
With the trust of the Lord
Trust him and your life will turn better afterwards.

Valence Festus (12)
St Joseph's Academy, Blackheath

Crime Does Not Pay

I used to be in a gang
I used to have too many fags
The day came when I had a fight
I reacted and pulled out a knife . . .

As I walk into the darkness and the shadows called my name
Rain pours down upon me once again I feel the pain
As tears roll down my eyes my life flashes by.

Prison was hard,
But my family sent me Christmas cards,
My first visitors were my mum and dad
Now they know I was bad.

They never knew I was hiding under a 'hood'
They thought I was good.
My dad said to me
Never to be mean.

I wish I could go back in time
And never do that crime
Now I know two wrongs don't make a right
So turn around and do not fight.

A few years later I was released
I was happy, so happy and pleased

When I went back to school
I looked like a fool
I thought to myself, I should have never taken that tool
I went to the loo
I saw my gang
They pulled out a gun, and it went bang, bang.

'Guns and knives take too much life'.

Mohamed Kallon (12)
St Joseph's Academy, Blackheath

Mystery Person

It's a person who is bright,
She cooks so right,
She is so light,
She is the number one person in the whole wide world.
I will never change her to no one
She respects and loves me
But I did something wrong she will get angry!

Adrian Masola (11)
St Joseph's Academy, Blackheath

The Way I See You

My every waking moment is filled with you
Butterflies in my stomach,
Smile on my face,
A glow in my heart,
Life is worth living because of you,
The good times we share,
After the bad times we grow
We share our love with pride
And respect each other's soul
We may not have much money
We don't wine and dine
Yet every time you touch me
My heart still shines
I'm so lucky to have found such a good time
Best friends, my soulmate.

Jade Reader
St Nicholas School, Southend-on-Sea

Valentine's Day

Early morning of Feb 14th
The lovers exchange a kiss
Breakfast in bed is what they'll get
That's something they'll never miss.

Today is the day of togetherness
Today is the day for love
Today is when lovers entwine
The symbol of this is a dove.

Hearts and pink everywhere,
The true meaning of valentine,
Is where two people love each other,
Hearts and kisses are the sign.

Heather Ragoonanan (11)
St Paul's Academy, Plumstead

What Love

Do not write simply
Because you have paper and pens
Write if you know the reason why.
You shouldn't write
Because you want to be loved.
You must write to love and live
Because only then can love be adored,
And your full heart on paper
Will be known by me
This makes my love more alive when seen.

Justina Ayowunmi Adu (15)
St Paul's Academy, Plumstead

The Heath Of Death

Upon the grassy fields of peace
A mockery was set.
Many men had many jobs
Of crafting, I will bet.
The carpenters of Plumstead,
Eltham, and around,
Were working very hard
To get the caskets bound.
And woodcutters were chopping
Oak and falling from disease
The plague was sweeping round and round
You'd drop after you'd sneeze.

The doctor would be round your house
With a beak for his mask
He'd bolt your door and paint it red
And make you pay the fees.

The coffins would be ready for the rich and able men,
But for the poor there was a mass grave big enough for ten.
Gold lettering on rich men's graves
A quick scrawl for the poor,
Five chariots and tombs for the nobles,
Poor families would get a door.

Joseph Stevens (12)
St Paul's Academy, Plumstead

Valentine

I can't send you roses nor fax you my heart
I would email your kisses but we would still be apart.
I love you to bits just wish you could see.
I thought I might tell you that you are the world to me.

Oliver Scorer (12)
St Paul's Academy, Plumstead

London

The day I went to London,
It was immersed with beauty.
The lovely Thames flowing through.
London, the paradise of flowers.
It is flourished with tall buildings.
The shining people and the smokeless air of London
Made me think that London was the heaven of love.
London glorified with scents.
The London Bridge saw the love of the people since it was built.
When I saw London, I saw Heaven in front of me,
In front of me.

Jerin Andrews (13)
St Paul's Academy, Plumstead

Shooting Star

At night,
The stars shine bright,
Don't you see them glow,
But sometimes don't you just wish,
The shooting star will show.

The way it twinkles in the sky,
Don't you see it twinkle high,
It twinkles everywhere,
Sometimes you hardly know it's there.

So if you make a wish upon a star
It will get you very far.

Tamara Carby (11)
St Paul's Academy, Plumstead

My Little Sister

My little sister is evil and mean,
She could really kick ass because
I know, I've seen.

She may be cute and sweet all around,
But trust me she will make you frown.

She's good around teachers and some of my friends,
But she could teach bullying if you know what I mean.

But in other ways I love her, you know,
Because she's my beloved sister and I will always know,
That I love her till the day I die,
And I truly know that she doesn't lie,
When she says 'I love you until the end of life.'

Nhien Le (12)
St Paul's Academy, Plumstead

Teachers

T eachers are amazing people
E ducating till 8.15am till 5pm
A stounding at their work
C hildren adore them for what they do
H elpful what they can do
E ncouraging to the pupils around them
R eading, writing, PE, there is a teacher for every subject
S pecial to people as others can't have them.

Rebecca Lee (11)
St Paul's Academy, Plumstead

My London

You are who everyone knows.
Like a rock star with unforgotten words.
I'm walking down your street,
Seeing people I'll never meet.
Wondering how you have grown,
Into something that we depend on.
Then I see you standing of a colour green,
Those passers-by budge into me.
My eyes change colour,
Like a moonstone ring.
Flash of moods run right through me,
You stand out like a beauty queen.
Big flashlights and this isn't a dream.
A dream is one you want it to be.
That is why you're my London in green.

Monika Kersnauskaite (13)
St Paul's Academy, Plumstead

London

Our great fair city
How I remember Thames the
Way you rushed at my feet
Like a breath of lemon air.
How you at me at three how
I remember it beautifully
I remember the rush of the people like pigeons flying
From a hunter without any warning.
That is my fair London city.

Ese Ojo (13)
St Paul's Academy, Plumstead

My Experience Of London

London
It is just so grey
The trains are packed to the rim.
I gave a sigh of relief when I got off the train
It was so busy on the station, people running for the bus or running
To get to work
We were in no hurry to get to my dad's workplace.
When we got to the train station it was not as packed.
The trains took too long, so we went outside and caught a taxi.
The first thing we saw was the grey building.
When we finished in my dad's workplace,
We went to St James' Park
It was lovely and green.

Fiona Arkins (13)
St Paul's Academy, Plumstead

Temptation

Intricate designs, weaving a song of illusion,
A hazy mist of dreams,
Clouding the truth,
Enhancing imagination.
The delicate twirl of skirts,
In an eternal dance.
More beauty than the sun itself,
Glowing with greed.
An elegant terror to tempt the world,
Like a diamond dagger.
Guilty innocence,
Honest lie.

Elizabeth Walker (11)
St Paul's Girls' School, London

Cold

The sun shone icicles,
And there I was,
Looking down on the world from my grassy perch,
The wind blowing the clouds from the sky,
And the fragments fell down to the Earth,
Cold as space.

I was walking,
Fragments of cloud in my hair,
Walking down to the world that lay at my feet,
The wind encouraging me down,
Wanting me to be out of its way.

I stumbled,
Increasing my speed down the hill,
Falling now, to the Earth I did not want to see,
I tried to put my feet on the ground
But fell faster down into the cold.

Kaarina Aho (11)
St Paul's Girls' School, London

Nature

A moment of warmth and peacefulness
Glowing ball of love and kindness
A thing of beauty and undisturbed tranquillity
Combination not a concoction
A natural occurrence not manmade
Perfectly created and smooth to touch
Earthy yet rounded
Something to treasure forever.

Anna Thomas (12)
St Paul's Girls' School, London

Losing A Friend

It can't have been long ago, those days
I can feel them so clearly
Creeping up quietly, so clear and so sudden
It might have been yesterday
Every time that I see your hair swinging ahead of me
In a corridor, next to some other
I wouldn't know what to say to remind you
Not any more.
And I can remember how -
Not at all long ago -
Our eyes could meet in gleeful understanding
Or in some little anguish
But you had to grow up, or maybe just distant
You talk to more eloquent people.
I raise my eyes to look at you now
And yours turn away.

Bethany Aitman (15)
St Paul's Girls' School, London

Mud Pies

I sent my little boy away,
To grab a gun, to go and play,
Make mud pies in the fields of France,
To see and leap at glory's chance -
Or that's what I thought yesterday.

Through the fire I saw his blood,
Oozing, mixing with the mud,
No head to crown with laurelled lies,
But in his hands were two mud pies,
Made for me, filled with his own blood.

Catherine Olver (13)
St Paul's Girls' School, London

The Daisy

Daisy, why a daisy?
On this chilly winter's morn,
Who picked out this flower?
Who froze it in bloom?
This crystallized daisy.

Not the dead rose I saw,
Nor the violet.
Only the daisy.
Why keep this daisy
And preserve it in ice?
Why not another?
Others are as fine as it.

Then the wind whispered in my ear
'I chose this daisy
I, Nature, Mother Nature
Chose this daisy,
To preserve it for evermore.

Not the rose
Nor the violet.
But this daisy,
This perfect daisy
With its pearly petals
And symmetry so fine.

I chose this daisy
For its simple grace.
No one sees me
But I am still here,
Overlooked like the daisy
But here nonetheless.'

Addy Young (12)
St Paul's Girls' School, London

Blind Man's Bluff

What does it feel like to walk around
Not knowing everyone's watching you?

I am different from everyone
Different as can be
Everyone has something I don't
Which is eyes that can see.

They play a game
Called hide 'n' seek
How can I seek
When I can't see?

I don't see who approaches me
I can't play games 'cause I need to see
Life is harder when you cannot peek,
With eyes that cannot see.

I see with my ears
Not with my eyes
Which is something I fear
If only I could fly.

Close your eyes
Walk around
See with your ears
Now you know it is to be a blind guy.

Maria Raji (13)
Sarah Bonnell School, Stratford

Life Through Someone Else

Looking through someone else's life
Is a dreaming secret.

I'm beautiful like the sun shining up in the sky
I travel everywhere with all the shining gold
I'm famous with the golden crown sparkling
I'm kind as the kittens, 'miaow, miaow!'
I'm a busy person throughout the day.

I help the poor and help others
My palace is huge just like the wonderland.
The new year appears with celebrations but
I only know that I'm beautiful and organised.
I travel everywhere around the world;
I'm the Queen of Everyland.

It's nice to see through somebody else's eyes.

Sophina Mahmood (13)
Sarah Bonnell School, Stratford

Life Through Someone Else's Eyes

Today I'm the person who I like
I'm so proud, I'm so nice
I'm the girl with all the good things
I'm so famous, I'm so pretty
I'm sitting on a sofa
Feeling alright
Then staring at the house
And saying oh my! then looking at my pictures and saying,
Is that me?
I'm so nice
I'm feeling really great
Now have not got much to say
Only that I'm a celebrity
I'm so famous and also really nice.

Gulshan Zahra (13)
Sarah Bonnell School, Stratford

Inside Out

I don't understand why they run away
I only tell the truth and they feel hurt and stay out of my way.
I may be popular but I feel alone
Sometimes I feel like running home
Nobody knows this and I'll make sure of that.

People see me as happy and fun, but I feel the opposite of that
However fun I may be I still have enemies that despise me
They try to break me down but I'll never fall,
I'm like a bird, I'm free.

I guess I take out my anger on smaller kids I think
I take their hurt to heal my pain
But all of this is in vain
For I know I'll never heal unless I leave and never come back.

Leave all of it behind me
Then I truly will be free
I admit my mistakes
And I am truly sorry.

Isabella Ismay (12)
Sarah Bonnell School, Stratford

Life As A Blind Person

Imagine being me,
Imagine not being able to see,
You walk around,
Not knowing what to do,
You can't see the cars,
The sun,
Never having light in your life,
All your life trapped,
Trapped in the dark,
Caught up all in bad thoughts,
Imagine being me,
Imagine not being able to see.

Sarah Vincent (13)
Sarah Bonnell School, Stratford

Seeing The World Through A Teacher's Eyes

I taught them how to read,
It was easy to lead,

Why is it so fun to teach,
Just like a healthy peach,

As soon as I step to my right,
They never started to fight,

They are always caring,
And always sharing,

I taught them new skills,
Also the story Jack 'n' Jill,

I've always been kind,
'n' easy to find.

Students I will always remember,
Just like a family member.

Ayesha Khanom (12)
Sarah Bonnell School, Stratford

Untitled

I am a servant in the 15th century
My life is cruel
And gruel.

I hardly get fed
And I don't have a bed.

I am lonely and poor,
I always get left at the door . . .

I am not rich, like some people you see,
I am poor, unwanted and left to make tea.

I never get noticed, I'm sad and poor,
But . . . why do I always get left at the door?

Ella Becket (13)
Sarah Bonnell School, Stratford

A Refugee - Why Me?

Scared and frightened,
All alone
I have no money, family
I have no home!

I've left my homeland -
Nothing but conflict and war,
Displaced and traumatised,
Please no more!

Seeking for refuge
I've fled to England,
Where everything's huge
Please accept me!

Dumb and worthless,
Is what I feel,
Down in my heart
It hurts a great deal.

Of all things
I'd love to be,
Like you - normal
Not a refugee!

Nadia Mumtaz Khan (15)
Sarah Bonnell School, Stratford

Life From Someone Else's Eyes

My world may be black, with nothing to see,
But I feel more than a normal person will feel.
I may be blind, I may be ugly,
But what matters is my heart is pure.
My family and friends are always there for me,
I'm never left out I am always a part of something.
So it doesn't really matter what you look like,
What your face looks like,
What really matters is the person you are inside.

Rezwana Akhter (13)
Sarah Bonnell School, Stratford

A Startling Experience

Imagine how life would be as a blind person?
Abandoned and frightening,
Mournful and despondent.

Imagine how I would be able to face the world?
With determination,
Or with desolation.

Imagine how I would be educated in school?
With special equipment,
Or a teacher to assist me.

Imagine how I would be treated?
With discourtesy,
Or with honour.

Imagine what I could be?
A doctor,
Or a blacksmith.

Imagine how the world would appear like?
Ravishing and clean,
Or unsightly and abhorrent.

Imagine how I would look?
Prepossessing or cute,
Or hideous and daunting.

Waseema Ahmed (13)
Sarah Bonnell School, Stratford

I Am A Refugee

I am a refugee!
I beg of someone to rescue me,
All scarred and shot; my hands and knees
That is why I seek for safety.

I am a refugee!
My last home was fiery,
My few belongings are tiny
That is why I seek for safety!

I am a refugee!
Roaming the deserts; lonely
I wish to be safe and free
That is why I seek for safety!

I am a refugee!
I am so very hungry
There is no food for me
That is why I seek for safety!

I am a refugee!
I have no parents to look after me
There is no one but me and this tree
That is why I seek for safety!

Help me! Save me! Rescue me!
I am a refugee
Please grant me security!

Yasmin Ahmed (13)
Sarah Bonnell School, Stratford

Deaf

People may think I'm different
But I'm just like them all,
People may make fun of me, may bully me
What really matters is the person I am.

You can bully me you can make fun of me
But you truly know I'm just like you,
I can't hear everything
You say, you may say bad things.

Things or good things
But that doesn't mean I haven't got any feeling,
So feel for everyone and treat them
As your equal because you know they are just like
You!

Zara Khan (13)
Sarah Bonnell School, Stratford

My Life

My life is like a river
It starts at one end and ends at another
My river has rapids, these are the troubles I may face.
My river has trees and frost,
These are like its friends and enemies.

The frost is its enemy, it makes the river feel cold and alone,
Miserable like it's just a bit of water.

The trees are its friend
Some are tall, funny and have golden leaves,
Some are small and quiet, and listen to the birds' sweet songs.

Altogether you may find a lot along the way,
But just remember when you're a river
There are ups and downs,
But when you're a waterfall there is no up, only down.

Sophie Davies (12)
Sir Charles Lucas Arts College, Colchester

The Girl Whose Only Best Friend Was An Old Teddy Bear

There was a little girl who lived all alone
Her dad was a drunk and her mum was an addict,
She lived in the attic at the top of the stairs
With only an old scraggy bear,
Which when she was one, she found under the stairs,
If only the parents cared about this five year old girl
She'd be happy instead of being alone.
She doesn't go to school and doesn't have any friends,
Her only one was the little old bear all worn and torn and once lived
In a box under the stairs.
This little girl lived a very sad life, if only she was loved,
She'd still be here.
She was beaten and bruised and lived in fear, of her mother mostly.
Then one day her mum came home, high on loads of drugs.
She turned to the girl and went to a drawer near by the door,
She pulled out a blade
One that she had made, it was pointy and sharp.
She turned back to the girl and thrust the blade into her skinny chest
She then walked out the room shouting,
'You deserve to die, you worthless pest.'
But when she was all by herself once again she did not fear,
As she gasped for breath she reached for the bear
Who once lived under the stairs.
When the police came it was far too late,
It then turns out that poor little girl bled to death
With her bear on her chest.
Her only friend was there till the end,
She rests in peace to this very day,
Thank God she left that scary place,
So now she has left but never had a chance to speak.

> So this is my poem and the morale is for more kids like her
> To speak out and have a chance to be heard . . .

Stephanie Nicholls (12)
Sir Charles Lucas Arts College, Colchester

My Life

It is a very hard life for me,
At school I get called names.
But the point that no one can see,
Is that it feels like people are hitting me.

At least I have friends
Who are as kind as they can be.
But sometimes we drive each other around the bend,
Even though we lose our key.

My mum loves me so much,
But I love her more.
Even though I feel like a bunny in a hutch,
I would give her a 10 score!

My form tutor is the best,
She has a nice smile.
I think she is better than the rest,
For her I would run a mile.

So that is my life,
A very short tale.
Oh, what a strife
I wish I could sail.

Coleen Armstrong (13)
Sir Charles Lucas Arts College, Colchester

My Tribute

The world is made up of anything everything has a role,
If anything were to go extinct
It would have to be humans not to be offensive at all.

There's a little ant, bug or bee disliked by everyone,
Everyone but me, there's a bird of prey
Not the best for taste,
Always approached with caution or haste.

If I were a fluffy animal like a kitten with its mum,
Even they can be hated by some,
Even if it was a big cat, wolf or bear,
I would just be killed for my beautiful hair.

But I am a human that loves all,
Animals, humans it doesn't matter to me at all,
But if I were to say thank you,
Thank you to anyone at all,
It would have to be the host,
My tribute is to Steve Irwin the hero who was lost.

Cherie Lovage (15)
Sir Charles Lucas Arts College, Colchester

The Eye Of The Universe

The eye of the universe holds no mercy.
Space and time lost in a sea of black.
Worlds and cultures captured forgotten.
Held in a prison that confuses science.

A strange paradox, endless and infinite.
Swirls, dips and dives.
A journey into the unknown.
Constellations, life and love. Lost. Taken.

A hungry soul, defying the laws of gravity.
Looking so peaceful, yet so destructive.
Beautiful yet deadly.
Mysterious, bewildering, a killer.

Bringer of the end.
A tunnel of time, gravity and pressure,
Leading to the realms of the lost.
Once inside, there is no escape.

A calm and brutal way to go,
Suspended in beauty and wonder.
Born from a star, to take its creator.
What does it hold? Heaven, Hell?

So silent still.
Magical.
Amazing.
Black hole, the eye of the universe.
It holds no mercy.

Melissa Walker (15)
Sir Charles Lucas Arts College, Colchester

Drug Misuse

You have somebody to turn to,
You always have done.
And yet you bottle it all up,
But you cannot hide, you cannot run.
The self harm was foolish,
What did you do that for?
I ask myself,
Will you do it anymore?
The amount of effort I have put into helping you,
Was it all worth it in the end?
Why do you hurt me so much?
The truth you like to bend.

After the first overdose, you didn't speak to me,
From fear of what I might say,
You are a wreck and a failure,
Do you really believe you are OK?
We want the best for you,
We all care about you mate,
You are selfish and stupid,
How did you get in this state?
So many lives are ruined this way,
Why do you hate life such?
The reason I am having a go,
Is because I care so much.

But then you let me down for the final time.
The overdose nearly killed you,
Everybody was in tears and I wouldn't sign the card.
Because all respect for you was then gone.
And you know exactly where you went wrong.

Michael Johnston (16)
Sir Charles Lucas Arts College, Colchester

A Teacher's Lament

You should have your homework,
There's no chance to debate it,
And there is no point in saying
That the blasted doggy ate it.
Enough of your if's,
Enough of your but's
Enough of your comments
And enough of your smut.
I just don't see why
You're falling behind,
I want to help you
I've tried and tried,
You're getting more like your brother
I remember him well,
If you don't want to be like him
Then start working like Hell.
Pull up your socks
And get your head down,
And we'll make a smile
Out of that frown.
That's all I have to say
And I won't say it again,
Now open your books
And take out your pen.

Samuel Lees (15)
Sir Charles Lucas Arts College, Colchester

Us

They want us to grow up,
But do we want to?
No!
We don't want to get a job yet,
Or a big house.
All we need is a decent rock to grow off,
All we need is to be *us,* yes ourselves!

They want us to be mature,
But do we want to?
No!
We don't need to be posh,
Or dressed up fancy.
All we need is to be well rounded in our own way
All we need to be is *us,* yes ourselves.

They want us to pay more attention to the world
But do we want to?
No!
We don't need to know about politics,
Or who's blowing up who.
All we need to know is that what we do now will
Shape it for us.

Adults just don't seem to understand us
What we do and what we say helps us
It's a youth thing, all the styles, it's for our benefit
All we want to do is to be us! Ourselves.

Jade Duller (13)
Tendring Technology & Sixth Form College, Clacton-on-Sea

Us

Us, together, as a human race,
Help to make the world move round,
Life and Earth move on,
But we move on with it,
Us, together, as a human race.

Us, together, as a country,
Strive to keep it running smoothly,
Time and country move on,
But we move on with it,
Us, together as a country.

Us, together, as a family,
Co-operate and care
People and relatives move on,
But we move on with them,
Us, together as a family.

Us, together as a couple
Live to love.
Love and bonds move on,
But we move on with them,
Us, together, as a couple.

Charlotte Luxford (14)
Tendring Technology & Sixth Form College, Clacton-on-Sea

Us

'There's six of us and only two of you!'
Said Biff, the school's big, burly bully.
Sue stepped forward, being the braver of the two,
'You're just dumb and think you're tough but you're not!'
Sue's friend Sarah stood and saw her friend's head
Being flushed in the loo.

Sue walked home battered and bruised,
Her bag was in tatters and her schoolwork was a mess,
She knew for a fact her mum wouldn't be amused.
Sue had to find a way to get her own back,
She would talk to the head of the school, she knew what to do.

The next day Sue and Sarah snuck into school,
Only because they were scared of Biff,
They did not want to run into him at all.
'Miss Hardman we need to ask you something,
We're being bullied by Biff and he is very cruel!'

A few hours later Biff was alone,
His group of cronies had all gone home.
However he was surrounded by a whole group of people,
And the only one in plain sight was Sue.
'How does it feel now there's ten of us and one of you?'

Sam Jones (14)
Tendring Technology & Sixth Form College, Clacton-on-Sea

Us

He was always there,
Always around
Always ready to make me smile,
He was always Rouse.

He would look into my eyes
And I would gaze into his
We would spend hours together
We could not be closer than this.

He was as old as I was
And I had never known a time without him by my side
But cancer took him away
And the pain I could not hide.

I wish it would go back,
To how it was before,
Where whenever I got home,
He'd be waiting at the door.

But things will never be the same
Because he's never coming back
And every time I hear his name
I hear my heart go crack.

He would always be happy to see me
And I would always make a fuss
As much as I miss him
I can't miss anything more than us.

He was more than just a dog
He meant so much to me
I would give anything
To just have one more moment
With my Rousey.

Jessica Webster (14)
Tendring Technology & Sixth Form College, Clacton-on-Sea

Us

A whole life of being single
And never finding the right guy,
Had caused a lovely young girl
To lay in bed at night and cry.

She searched high and low around her school
For a boy that caught her eye,
She wanted love at first sight
When the sparks start to fly.

She changed her hair, she straightened it
To see if she had a chance,
Just to walk past a group of boys
With not a single glance.

So back at home she cried again
Her mascara running down her face,
She wished she could evaporate off the Earth
Without leaving anyone a trace.

'You'll find the right man in time'
Her mother and father had said,
She still hoped and prayed to be loved
With her parents' voices in her head.

She made friends with a lot more boys
As the days went on and on,
'Maybe,' she thought, 'This could be
My chance to find the perfect one.'

And so she did, she found a man
He gave her lots of attention and made a fuss,
And finally, happily, she could safely say,
'It's not me, it's us.'

Terri-Leigh Waters (13)
Tendring Technology & Sixth Form College, Clacton-on-Sea

Us

I am Claire and my sister is Emily,
I am 13 and she is 11.

I am intelligent and so is she,
What a blow that can be!

Me and my sister are like two peas in a pod,
We are scissors chopping each other apart.

We are stray dogs pining for attention,
Luckily neither of us have had a detention.

Me and my sister are like a pair of antagonistic muscles,
When one gets angry, the other relaxes.

We have a fun but stressful time,
We work together well in rhyme.

Half of the time we argue,
The other half being nice sisters.

We are two miaowing cats fighting in an alley,
A calm river floating through the valley.

Me and my sister sometimes share,
Other times our own is our own.

It doesn't help when our birthdays are near,
Wishing they weren't at that time of year.

We are careful and helpful,
Long-lost friends.

I suppose we love each other really,
Obviously, well nearly.

Claire Hills (13)
Tendring Technology & Sixth Form College, Clacton-on-Sea

Us

In the morning
In the night
We are together
Never one of us out of sight.

All of us
Stand side by side
Waiting patiently
For time to pass by.

We stay hidden
We stay in the dark
Waiting intently
For the gentle song of the skylark.

As time passes by
In the light of the moon,
I say to myself,
We will escape from this soon.

Each and every person,
Fails to see,
The truth about us
And the answer to,
Who are we?

Daniel Wall (13)
Tendring Technology & Sixth Form College, Clacton-on-Sea

Haunted House

The doors will creak wherever you go,
The ghostly spirit glides through the window
Run from the skeletons in the hall
The bloodthirsty bats are worst of all.
You run for your life, there's no way out.
You scream your loudest and try to shout.
The bats will find you wherever you hide.
Once they spot you, they go out of their mind!

Atlanta Knight (11)
The Compton School, London

Darkness Of Depression

I am the shadow,
Afraid of the sun,
I live in the darkness,
With absence of fun.

When you're trapped with me,
You'll disappear,
The people I've snatched,
Would not volunteer.

Nightmares will haunt you,
And gloom will soon follow,
No cure but sweet chocolate,
Fills a hole this hollow.

There are medicines to help you
But I will not go
When I have you, I'll keep you
On your face it will show.

You will be my prisoner
And people will see
They'll know what you suffer
And that you're not free.

I feed on misery,
I'm born with pain
No physical symptoms
No pleasurable gain.

Turning you cold
Tears spring from your eyes
They fill up your world -
Water-filled skies.

I'll dominate you all
Leave you emotional and upset
Mentally disturbed
Wishing time would reset.

Cheryn Jordon (10)
The Compton School, London

Shushhh . . .

It's just conflict after conflict,
War after war,
But Tony Blair sits in his chair
And demands some more.

He has a friend, does old Blair,
He's called Mr Bush
And Mr Bush has some friends,
But their countries are being smooshed.

There are adults and seniors, babies and kids,
They all try to recover,
But then another bomb hits.

'Why,' we all ask,
'Do Mr Bush and Mr Blair,
Not put a stop to this terrible affair?'

Well the truth is, my friends,
We know a bit too much, about old Bush,
For if he knew we know about his *secret* friends,
He'd tell us to shush.

'I'm the ruler of the country,' he'd tell us with glee
'But if you mess up my status, I'll have to live in poverty!'
Mr Bush won't be so happy now!

'Then so it will be,' we will tell him with anger,
'For there are so many families who are dying of hunger!'

'You don't understand,' Mr Bush will plead,
'Please don't deny me something I really, really need!
I can't change my ways, it will be the end of my days!'

'It will be the end of your days, whatever you choose,
Mr Bush and Mr Blair,
'Don't sit there hiding behind your old chairs!'

Radha Bhatt (12)
The Compton School, London

The Horrors Of War

Guns howl with rage as they murder innocents.
Men flee in vain as bullets riddle them with holes.
Shellshock rules the bloodstained ground.
Mines blast men to smithereens and corpses litter the earth.
The seas turn red as flamethrowers sear the flesh of soldiers.
The souls of the dead whisper in the whistling wind.
Bombs fall from the sky and destroy all in their path.
Blood scatters across the land and bones are turned to dust.
Brains fly through the air, limbs are lost and guts lay bare on
the floor.

All this for what,
For the honour of a country?
For the lives of the people?
For survival and an end to famine?
Or for the end of racism and discrimination?

Lyuben Vachkov (12)
The Compton School, London

Father To Son

Well son, life as we know has
Been very hard for me and you,
Since we've never known what to
Do with our lives. You have to try, not
Me, I've already have completed my life
Changing journey, keep on trying
Never give up
Always remember that I'm always
In your heart.
Always have a caring mind but
Never trust someone with just one keen eye.

Have a good start to life not one without
Any light. One more thing
Before we move on the light and the
Dark will never come unite as one.

Kareem Marsh-Henry (11)
The Compton School, London

A Sinful World

What a beautiful world we live in!
Rivers of blood,
Dark clouds of smog,
And smoking craters where cities once were.

What a wonderful world!
Corrupt rules,
Weak leadership and greed.

This planet is great!
A black sun and a red moon,
Scorched women and children
Burnt by the sun,
And melted ice and rising waters.

Human kind is making a real breakthrough!
While wars are fed,
People starve,
And the world is governed by vengeance.

They say, 'an eye for an eye'
But eventually the world will go blind.

Gabriel Akamo (12)
The Compton School, London

Night Dreams

Snow is sparkling in the night
Treasure growing in the light
Dream of lovely things I might
Nearly morning but not quite.

Wake up early in the morning
Watch the sun as it is dawning
Red clouds mean a shepherd's warning
Stretch my arms and can't stop yawning.

Jordan-Louise Day (11)
The Compton School, London

Race On A Face

As I stand on this pitch,
I know there's at least one racist pig
In England there's race,
On every different face
One of them at least,
Feeling anger towards this
So many murders,
Going further and further
Just to hurt one another
Because of their father and mother
Uniting together to make yet another
Race on a face
With each look there's pain
Some look in vain
Some walk the streets
Having not met before,
But they will once more
As the world is small like a herd of sheep on one big ball
Parents making babies,
All different races
Some bilingual showing their racial features,
To all other people.
Together we join
Hand in hand throughout time
To make more race
For each single face,
Which equals yet another,
Race on a face.

Charlotte Copeland (16)
The Compton School, London

Love

Once in a lifetime it comes
Only from your loved ones
Who are they you ask
Well this is what I say.

Mums, dads, and all your family
Boyfriends, girlfriends and all your partners
Wives, husbands and everyone you know
Friends, enemies all in one go.

Once in a lifetime it comes
Only from your loved ones
What do you do to show your love you ask
Well this is what I say at last.

Give a hug or handshake and do this every day
Make a promise and then don't let it sway
Never betray and always show you care
Think of what it would be like without them and if you could bare.

Once in a lifetime it comes
Only from your loved ones
What do you give to them you ask
Well this is what I say at last.

Care, support and your love back
Help, friendship and never slack
Loyalty, commitment and never give up
Hope, smiles and all the effort you can chuck.

So now the end,
I hope you've learnt
What love is and how it's earnt.

Linda Epstein (11)
The Compton School, London

The Death Of Youth

A mobile phone, glued to the hand
of a girl so innocent and young
is enough to witness her chatter, talking just like
a teenage moron from a soap opera
despite being eight years old. As we follow our
everyday lives we are already
in an adventure of ignorance without warning.

But it does not matter to everyone else;
Only to those with a view and a belief.

Mature clothing, wrapped around the body
of a little child with adult tastes is enough
to describe her like a stereotype on the streets.
Those who talk and walk cliché,
thinking they are 18, not 8. We are in this climax
of a tale in which we are too shocked . . .
to speak.

But it does not matter to everyone else;
Only to those who are worried and concerned.

Dolls, released on the market,
Are not really dolls at all. These
'Dolls' have their adult handbags, their adult
mascara and their adulterated
catchphrases.
They have thrown away childhood;
thrown away innocence that we are
supposed to enjoy.
This venomous, manipulative
doll just for a company to bathe in money.
It already has the power to hypnotise.

But it does not matter to everyone else;
Only true people who know better and have common sense.

A martian walking back home
in a hood, is ten years old and already
smoking the maturity from a cancer stick,
acting tough, drunk on power
and trading his health and self away.
Just to be a stereotype.

And with his knife, stained from the red
blood of innocence looks around the cold,
dull dark streets. The martian thinks that
he has finally grown up, away from his childhood
when he sees a hardworking somebody pass by.
The lethargic and careless 'mini adult'
pollutes the air with his own strong language
and smoke in front of the somebody.
The hardworker ignores him and blocks out the noise because

As I said: the death of youth does
not matter to everyone else;
But when the knife finally strikes

Down, it will.

Tom Heritage (16)
The Compton School, London

World War II

The wailing of the dying volunteers,
The guns going bang, bang, bang
Hundreds of families have lost one more member,
Soldier's bravery being tested once more.

Once they're gone; dead but not forgotten.
The country full of fear not knowing if they would die.
Trying to think positively but it is harder than they thought,
Wishing they could see into the future to see if they were alive.

Their heart beating as fast as an Olympic runner,
Their friends next to them one minute; on the floor the next,
Wondering if their companions are dead or just hiding away,
Going through each day with fear.

Every single bomb is an evil enemy,
The rivers of blood flowing down to the sea from all the dead bodies,
The ruthless tanks destroying everything in their path,

Waiting, wishing, wondering, when the war would cease,
Hoping the world would soon come to peace.

Emma Goldsmith (12)
The Compton School, London

This Madness

What is this desperate madness; what is this burning hell?
The tortured cry of humanity, rotting away in the dust?
Does wrack my ears, this grievous story that I tell,
There is nothing anymore that is just.

For if there is a no truth to be told,
If the lies are allowed to roam free,
These lies of many centuries old,
Will purge this sanctuary.

See the eternal soldier who weeps bitter tears,
For the madness that we fill our world with,
In a forever of years
Nobody can live.

Blood is like black fire;
Black fire is shod on the battlefields.
The putrid odour of burnt nitre,
Will never ever yield.

The bullets whistle by,
Always; always.
Why?
Death waits for us as sure as every bird does fly.

The rapid ruthless relentless report of the guns; the endless pain,
Never will this madness end.
For every dead noble soldier who died in vain,
There are a million billion bystanders massacred.

The grenades:
A lifetime of endurance; *bang!*

This madness shall surely be:
The destruction of us all.

Harlan Kohll (13)
The Compton School, London

Protest poem

Look at you
Standing there laughing
Because he is disabled.

Explain to me,
Why do you do it,
And how is it funny?
Would you like experiencing their pain?
What if your friend breaks their leg,
Are they disabled?
Would you laugh at them,
Lying there in agony?
How is it funny?
Watching someone who is less well off than you,
Who has a disability?
So tell me,
How would you feel,
If someone laughed at you?
Did your parents bring you up to be like . . . this?
To laugh because someone does not function the same as you?
Well get this
They do on the inside.

On the inside,
The people you laugh at,
Are better than you,
They take what they have been given,
Pleased just to be living,
But people like you abuse it and take it for granted

So have some respect,
Be grateful
And when you do you will know who you truly are . . .

Anthony Sturt (14)
The Compton School, London

Life Is A Jungle

Life is a jungle,
Never a safe moment,
Nowhere to hide,
Nowhere to escape to,
Got no water,
Got no food,
Wherever the way out is,
You'll find it,
I know you can,
I'm sure you can,
Just keep goin',
You stay up,
Stay fit,
Stay motivated,
To fight off the jungle,
To get on top of the jungle,
All you got to do is keep on goin'
Just keep goin'
Carry on from where I left,

You can fight the jungle,
Even when it's hard,
You'll get past the sinking sand,
When you get lost and the muddy paths,
You'll make it eventually,
Just you wait,
You can do it,
Because life is a jungle.

I have used the metaphor 'jungle'
Because a jungle has loads of things
Along the way that is hard to cross
And so has life,
I used this kind of structure
Because the poem 'Mother to Son'
(by John Agard) inspired me.

Sh'kyra Jordon (11)
The Compton School, London

The Terrors Of War

The war was dreadful
As soon as we hit land
The bullets screeched as they
Pierced our skins.

The blood in the sea was as red as roses
The blood is a cool red drink
As we ranted and raged
To fight for our country
You could see people
Screaming
And screeching for their lives.

The guns shouted
The bombs blasted
People looked terrified as the
Ranting roaring raging rifles screeched
As they flew through the air.

The fire is burning
Our lives flashed before our very own eyes
To be home and safe is our only desire
We know we might not see our family again.

The pain we are all in is excruciating
We cry as we see our mate's life being blasted away
The soldiers crying is as bad as listening
To the same song over and over again.

Another scream
It was like a baby crying for more attention
We see our soldiers lying there
Dead on the floor
We've signed up now
What's done is done.

Hayley Mansfield (13)
The Compton School, London

I'm Sorry

I'm sorry
Dressed in different clothes
So I'm emo.

Well I'm sorry
But why do you label me
And call me emo?
Do you mean I can't control my emotions
And all I can do is cry
Always apathetic
I'm sorry
But why do you label me?
Do you mean I have no friends?
They all reject what I've become
A body missing a soul
Well therefore
Everyone
Is missing a soul
Some of them don't even know
That their emotions are missing
So unaware, so cold
So 'Emo'
I'm sorry
But why do you label me
And call me emo?
Is it that my clothes aren't spectrum?
Blue, red, green, yellow,
Black.
The one at the end of the line
Of every line
The absent colour that is always there.

I'm sorry
Why do you label me?
Am I too emotional to listen to you
Listening to nothing
Only focusing on the morbid
Feeding off the bad thoughts
That spiral through my head
The pain that courses through my veins
Because my life is just a black abyss

And I'm too cold
Too sad
Too emotionless
To care what you're saying
Tomorrow isn't another day
It's another battle
To find people to understand me
So maybe tomorrow you'll understand
Maybe you won't
But just maybe
Not that I can understand possibility.

But I'll try to explain
I have other feelings
I'm only human.

Kathryn Davies (15)
The Compton School, London

An Asian Girl

There's more people like me
An Asian girl
Who likes to dance.
Who's going to prance
Up and down.
Who is proud to be an Asian girl?
I am hip hip hooray!
I'm proud to be my culture
But I'll still be me.

Though I'll let time pass me by.
As I know there's more people like me
An Asian girl!
I love my Asian food
As I won't put up my hood
As I'm proud to be me
Everyone says it loud and proud
An Asian girl!

Manshi Patel (12)
The Compton School, London

The Great War

A great war has begun,
In the age of the Shogun,
Thousands of fearless warriors
Preparing to shatter
The enemy barriers.

The Japanese leader
Was very brave,
He said he will bring the enemy to their grave,
With his Chaotic Sword he slaughtered all
The enemy was beginning to fall.

The Japanese leader was a wild bear,
Dragging and killing the enemy in his lair,
The enemy leader lost his weapons,
He was clawless
The Japanese were very flawless.

He won a great war,
And thanked the gods on the seashore.
He thanked his fighting samurais
And rewarded them with some nice baked pies.

Christopher Aradipiotis (11)
The Compton School, London

Difference

Are we so different after all?

We wear these clothes on our back,
Simply to keep us warm,
We listen to such different music,
But you can't deny they're all of equal art form
Yet there is divide
There is prejudice
There is something deeply gone wrong
All because
Of the need to belong.

Imagine a world,
Where people are disliked not for what they like
But for what they *are* like
Where disagreements arise not over how they dress
But how they address one another.

But to simply put it
If you were to cut us open
Our blood would be the same colour
If you were to cut us open
Deep inside, we're just the same as each other.

. . . Are we so different after all?

Louis Phillips (15)
The Compton School, London

Discrimination

Look at me . . .
Look at yourself
Are we really that
Different?

What is the need for racism?
Or even sexism?
Discrimination -
Discriminating someone
Because of the way
They look or speak?

What is so different
About each one of us?
Do you not have hair . . .
Or eyes . . .
Or even a nose or mouth . . .
Maybe you don't have ears . . .

Well so what . . .
Why put someone down
When it is the way they are -?

Why . . .
Disabled . . .
Able . . .
Weak . . .
Strong . . .
But you know that . . .
You are yourself.

No matter what you
Are . . .
Be yourself
And if anyone . . .
Anyone
Tries to make you
Change

Then say no
You are what you
Are

Your own person
Individual character
Be yourself
Never change
For anyone.

Jade Bazzoni (15)
The Compton School, London

Winter Has Come . . .

I'm angry when summer changes,
The sun hides its face,
The sun is no more,
It's a disgrace.

The snow falls,
The sun hides its face,
The rain pours down,
It's a disgrace.

No more ice creams,
The sun hides its face,
No more swimming,
It's a disgrace.

Summer has gone,
The sun hides its face,
There's nothing I can do,
Winter has come . . .

Sophie Mayer (11)
The Compton School, London

Mums At War

The bangs and crashes
Of the exploding bombs
All their lost ashes
So many grieving mums.

My son's out there
In the aim of the fire
I'm very aware
Their eyes are never drier.

Every soldier
Marching like they are in a trance
There arms and legs aching
Only with one chance.

The screaming bombs
Like crying babies
Deafening the men
But no apologies.

The pain always shared
Sad, scared and never safe
No one ever prepared
For the doom that awaits.

The women at home
Working like ants
No place to roam
Never with assistance.

Working in the fields
Looking after the young ones
Having to be their own shields
Having their daughters but never their sons.

The thousands of graves
Standing like the men they used to be
They had worked like slaves
To their country.

The parents all frozen
Like statues grieving
All of them chosen
Now they are leaving.

Lauren Juzl (12)
The Compton School, London

Proud To Be A Londoner

To jump up and down,
In a place in the city,
To run and scream,
And be paid a fair kitty.
Then travel home,
All safe and sound,
In my home, which cost lots of pounds.
Cos a Londoner I am . . .
And that's who I'll be forever.

To jump up and down,
In a place in the city,
Dance! jump up! and down!
Till the evening comes by,
Rest at pale evening,
In a big comfy bed,
As night come tenderly,
A Londoner, like me.

Sheena Shah (12)
The Compton School, London

Why Did They Do It?

The guns pointing at the enemy as he starts to pull the trigger
The bullets are magnets, charging at the enemy full of so
much force

Him and many others risking their lives
Everyone at home hoping he survives.

Bang bang another man down
As the shooting shout of the guns just carry on
While they're in the sea they start to drown
Their blood spreading round making the waves red
As the rest lay in agony and pain.

Boom boom goes the belch of the bomb
Another few men gone
They're like fireworks getting lit
But the roaring rounds of the bombs keep going on.

These courageous men are like the heroes for our country
They all fought in the war
Joy and happiness is what they did it for.

Tulsi Hirani (12)
The Compton School, London

Trip On The Ocean Of Life

Life is a boat trip on the ocean waves,
Sometimes it's nice and sunny just floating in your boat
In the big blue ocean,
But most of the time it's a rough ocean with storms and tidal waves,
But still you've got to enjoy life,
Those days on the calm ocean waves,
But fight those stormy horrible days,
Fight through them,
So don't turn back,
Keep on going on the journey of life,
But remember life isn't an easy ride,
And remember we're always there for you.

Alexander Tzortzi (11)
The Compton School, London

World War II

War on terror never ending
They step out and *bang!* they're down;
Another mother who's lost her boy
Tanks as big as hot air balloons
It is a living hell
The bullets roaring towards you
Wanting to knock one of our soldiers down once again.

There is skin red as roses,
As the blood is pouring out their hearts
Guns going rat-a-tat-tat
The hills break down into tears
The bombs blasting like fireworks in the dark moonlight
The soldiers crawling on the floor like little babies
Boom boom! Their bombs belch again

The night falls so the soldiers have rest
Just a few hours until it starts again
Scared to get out fighting for their country
Trying to survive but just missing the chance.

Dawn comes so the whole dying thing starts again
The terrified people wanting to survive
Bang! Down go a few more soldiers
But why?
Did they look like chickens or something?
Trying to kill them like butchers do
Well they should know that they were human beings as well;
Not just them!
We have sensitive feelings as well, like every other living being
So know how many people risked their lives,
For their own country
So now it's up to you if you want to fight for *your* country
The decision is in your hands.

Priyanka Depala (13)
The Compton School, London

The Gate

Day after day, year after year,
There's always a locked gate in front of us
You're on the safe side,
Protected from hurt
But, I'll always be on this side that'll rust.

As long as I'm on this side,
I won't know if I belong
The way that you treat me, is it right or wrong?

This gate made of paper
Is discreet like me, invisible but there
You try and destroy it
It won't collapse
Because our strength inside won't care.

As long as I'm on this side,
I won't know if I belong
The way that you treat me, is it right or wrong?

I'll help you find what you want,
To open the gate and forever it'll be gone.
If I won't be there
Neither will the gate
I won't be there anymore
It will be done.

As long as I was on that side,
I wouldn't have known if I belonged.
The way you treated me, was it right or wrong?

Delaram Ranaei (15)
The Compton School, London

Death Is Horrific

I hear the snapping of the guns
The boom of the bombs
I am afraid to poke my head above the trench
Afraid of what may happen
Afraid

I clamber over the trench
Eyes closed like a newborn baby
I scuttle to my place
Hoping I will survive, maybe, just maybe
Another soldier solemnly slumped before me, he is a frail insect
Begging for his life.

I shoot my weapon of death spitting its ammo
I blindly blast bombs scared to open my eyes
To see the horrors I have made real
Called into action
We run, scuttle and crawl as if we were tiny mice afraid of the
Cannon, guns and grenades

We run into the enemy head on like two blind ants
Daga daga daga
The blistering sound of the guns surrounds us, we call for back up
No one answers
No one comes

I turn around pushed in my face was the gaping mouth of the cannon
Stunned, not knowing what to do next
Boom, my head bursts into flames as I shout my last commands
Death *is* horrific.

Joshua Wood (12)
The Compton School, London

War

Why is there war, why is there pain?
Why can't there be love and peace again?
People are dying everywhere, why can't you help us
President Bush or Tony Blair?
Don't just sit there sipping your wine
As we don't have that much time
Bang, bang, bang, that's all there is
But won't it be nice to have a kiss, kiss, kiss
But you don't care, tell us the truth, all you care about is your
Family and you
Never mind about the rest of us
So tell us why we should keep your trust?
So give us a reason, give us one now, a good sensible reason
That would make us proud.
But you can't can you, not one single one as you are selfish and
Careless, and I don't give a damn
As long as you get your fruit scones with cream and jam
Or your 'cheeseburgers' or 'hamburgers' with some ketchup on
the side,
Which will make you huge and wide.
Anyway that is enough from me, as I have to go to help raise money
For charity.

Louise Medwicz (14)
The Compton School, London

Second World War

The war begun in 1939;
All those people fought for England and USA;
All those men were as brave as a super hero,
Lots of them died for their beloved region.
The guns fired; the roaring sound was a massive
Bang!

The enemy was Germany, they didn't care
For all their friends that died, and that shows how
Selfish they are.

The angry tanks shoot out the missiles killing and hurting
Everyone in its path.

The war is daunting and the soldiers are afraid
Because they might fear what is coming their way;
Brothers writing letters for their family and friends,
Saying goodbye and praying as well.

After the war finished everyone that survived were grateful
To all their friends and brothers for fighting as well,
They won all of them, were as happy as they will ever be,
Some were sad because a loved one died;
And that shows how war is bad.

Michelle Rodriguez
The Compton School, London

I Don't Know

Give it or I'll stab you
Just give it
That's what they said.

I don't know
What are you looking for?
An MP3?
A CD player?
A life?
I don't know
Why are you treating
Me like this?
What are you going to do?
A life is not worth
Taking for a petty thing
I don't know
Who are you?
A man?
A bully?
A killer?
Make up your mind
I don't know
Why are you doing this?
For fun?
As a dare?
To get by?
I don't know
Search me
You won't find
Anything even
Look

I don't know
Would your hero
Do something like this?
Would they
Or would they
Just try and get by?
I don't know.

I don't know
Why do you choose
Me
Me of all people?
Is it because
I have something
You want?
Do you just
Want a friend?
There are
Plenty more fish
In the sea
And lots more opportunities.

So make your
Decision
Are you able to kill or will you let me go?

Thomas Woods (15)
The Compton School, London

Concentration Camps

Locked up controlled, hidden,
Our life torn apart.
Our enemies never forgiven.
Concentration camps they're called;
Hell, death and pain;
The persecuted deem this a more accurate name.
Every day we see their face
In memories, around the place
But never in person theirs never a trace
Of the people you love maybe never again
Slam clash every morning is our alarm
Our lives are like a time bomb; *tick tick tick:*
Bang and you're gone
Notorious nasty Nazis choose who lives or dies.

Flash our life is before our eyes we are as scared as
                                        a screaming child.
A gun roared like an angry lion,
That's another man who had had enough who chose to give his life;
Rather than stay one more night
Men as dirty as chimney sweeps;
Children as innocent as Little Bo Peep;
Women who wouldn't harm a soul;
Have been in such conditions in such foul.

Germans vs English every war is the same,
Politicians treat it all as if it were a big game
It's not. It's death all in one word!
Pain hardly gain for the ones doing the work
War is wrong all it does is destroy!

Chloe Taylor (12)
The Compton School, London

Dream Flowers

Flowers are my sunshine,
But sometimes they are my rain.
Sometimes warm but then so cold.
It's a petal full of dreams,
Where some fall off and grow back on.

When the sun sets down,
And ocean is calm.
The moonlight shows warmth and comfort.
So the dreams of desires
Are ready to become reality.

The thin layer of moon,
Covers the flower in a delicate blanket
And where the sun is waiting to rise
Where it brings happiness and love to the world.

The sun rises up,
It brings a smile to the flower, trees and birds of sweetness
Happiness spreads around
Excitement in the puffy clouds.
Stars are hiding behind the moon
Giggling
And waiting till they come out
To enjoy the dreams of darkness.

Pink petals
Warming up my heart
Its precious colours are like a valuable crystal.

Its delicate softness and beauty
Being shared by the trees, and birds
Friendship grows and brings new colours into my life!

Ashita Gaglani (12)
The Compton School, London

A Trust Betrayed At The Dawn Of War

World War II
You people died for your country,
To think of them is to think of you,
The screeching sounds of soldiers,
Fire surrounding like hell,
The unthinkable temper of the bombs,
Plunging down like droplets of rain.

Innocent civilians gassed to their death,
My people surely didn't deserve this,
Why do wars have to be set on violence?
Maybe everyone could just be in peace . . .
Germany attacked like an infuriated lion,
Whilst England fought for six years
Continuously.

Bang! Boom! Bash!
The aeroplanes land with such a crash,
The land is like a graveyard.
The naked trees stir with the wind,
The roars of the guns,
The bawling of the sliced up soldiers
War, there's nothing good to set eyes on
War is a disease.

War is an unbearable plunge into disaster,
The war is like an attack from a shark,
Once it bites you can't let go!
Isolated soldiers waited for their deaths,
Weeping in the depths of a murky mouldy ditch;
Filled with the remains of rotting corpses,
Oh what a severe way to waste six years of combat.
Many people watched their men die
In the black of the night.

Suddenly everything's gone quiet,
Many souls have left,
You close your eyes and open them again,
And you realise the war is at end.
You've lost your companions; your men
By your side, and on your way to freedom,
The earth's great hunger of dead corpses
Swallowing bodies as they are buried
At their funerals for years and years . . .

The immorality of war.

Gandom Chavoushi (13)
The Compton School, London

My War Poem

World War II
You hear gunshots of brave soldiers fighting and defending
Bang! you see dying civilians lying on the floor so helpless:
The unbearable screaming soldiers dying and paramedics rushing
To them
Crash! the tree collapsed as the tank went *bang!*
The fingers of the trees covered many of the dead bodies
They died with their dignity;
I ran as I saw I was in a battleground
The tanks were as big as buses but it was outnumbered by many
Grenades
I walked forward and I saw polluted water saturated by blood;
You walk and you see shattered glass shiny as silk
The sound of angry guns sounding louder by the minute
The soldiers were as cunning as a fox
War is a disease killing after killing
Guns are diseases killing after killing.

You see your friend's exquisite faces
The six years of agony was over;
But the price for this was a lot of lives.

Nickul Bhagat (12)
The Compton School, London

Untitled

Animals are cute
Animals love you
Animals like everyone but maybe not you
Animals have memories
Just like you
Animals love toys
They bark from a noise
They are really cuddly
They are always happily playful
They may bark at you
Don't think they're going to bite you
Because they're not
Dogs hate cats
They always want to fight
They have too many memories
But may give you a fright
They jump up at you
They may lick you
They will not harm you
Unless you make them angry.

Sharelle Bello (12)
The Compton School, London

Friends Are . . .

Friends are here, friends are there
Friends are there when you marry a bear
Friends are there for you to care
Friends are . . .

Friends are there when you feel sad
Friends are there when you go mad
Friends are there to make you glad
Friends are . . .

Friends are there for you to play
Friends are there when you go your way
Friends are there every day
Friends are . . .

The reason why I chose this poem
Is because it is funny and it rhymes.
The poem 'Friends' make the reader
Think about what friends do for you
And how they help you.

Tasnim Rahman (11)
The Compton School, London

World War II

Bang bang twenty-four-seven
People living on rations
Innocent lives going to Heaven
Soldiers dying with passion.

You hear soldiers screaming in agony;
The tanks roaring as a great big lion;
No sign of harmony
The devastation of those whom being shot.

The guns stuttering
Soldiers battling in France
The enemy creeping up behind you
Could be your last chance.

Bullets flying everywhere
Destruction throughout the city
No sign of peace anywhere
Nowhere to run or hide.

Every soldier is an enemy;
The commander ordering you like a slave
Playing guns like a five year old boy
You've got to stand there and be brave.

Jignesh Ramani (13)
The Compton School, London

War On Terror

Innocent people have angry guns to their heads
And die; for no reason at all
You see people's eyes weep like waterfalls
While the soldiers think they're at war
Strong and scared bombs placed secretly
Alone and not to be found
Each has a big bang in-between
This is triggered without a sound
Bang boom bang!
The strong bombs screamed
Like fireworks in the dark sky
Next million lives lost
The knocked over and hurt train's stuck
Underground with people inside not to be found
It is hell in there and silent now
All the survivors are in shock but most of them
Destroyed
Why are these lives lost?
Why? Why? Why?
I know why
It's the people in Iraq whose loved ones have died
Why?
I don't know
That's for you to find out
Keep asking around and the truth will soon come out.

Shayan Ansari (12)
The Compton School, London

Hurricane

Like a hurricane
You swirl in my head,
Where my thoughts scream,
And my feelings run wild.
This feeling -
People call it love,
I could describe it
In so many ways.
The ability to frustrate - yet be forgiven.
To be frustrated - yet smile.
To cry - but never feeling sad.
Never feeling alone.
Paranoia makes me scream.
This sudden dependency
Was never here before.
Don't leave me, don't ever leave me.
I want to run
But stay with you.
I want to cry - and laugh
I want to get lost in
My new feelings.
I never knew feelings like this.
I never knew this feeling -
Sad, deflated - alone.
On my own
Life just isn't life
I no longer wish,
Wish, to live
And now
Those three scars bleed.

Saloni Chamberlain (16)
The Compton School, London

The Tragic WWII

I saw it from my own eyes; it took me by surprise,
Blood and bodies everywhere I couldn't look I just couldn't bear.
People screaming crying for help, but I just had to save myself,
As I was running I was looking back, I saw one soldier taking
Off his hat.
Bang, bang, bang the guns cruelly took him down; the bullet flew
Through his head
People are crowding around.

Fears in their eyes we have to carry on let's do it for our country
Let's be strong;
Rocks on the floor and broken glass, everyone was like a cheetah
Running extremely fast.
People were praying on their knees, I was murmuring aloud
Screaming, 'Please, please, please.'
All of the bodies scattered round all as silent as a mouse,
Another graveyard of bodies has been made,
Babies screaming frightened as a little lamb, 'Shhhhh,'
Mummy's saying, there goes another bang.
Some fear for forgiveness but they have to do it, do it for their country
You can see in their eyes they're really sorry,
I wish my guardian angel was here; to pick me up to take away
My fear,
To say it's OK to wipe my tear to be with me and to be near.
At last this tragic war has ended, but it's scarred me for life,
And it can't be mended.
I want to go home, but I don't know where to go,
Should I turn west I'll try and do my best,
My mum and dad would have wanted me to,
I wish this whole nightmare wasn't so true.
I know they'll be looking down on me,
And I feel so heartbroken and sorry.

Amy Matthews (13)
The Compton School, London

Fear Of Death

It started but never ended, it's like Hell but less gruesome.
Soldiers standing strong and proud like loyal dogs.
But know death is here and near,
still standing ready for commands.
Though Arab and Israeli are foe.
They still fear one death
because you know it's near.

On 1967 also known as 'Six Day' war, Arab on one side and Israeli
on the other.
Pointing guns at each other
even though they show no fear,
inside they feel fear
because they know now death is here.

They fire and all you hear is *bang, bang*
the bullets scream with anger as they charge;
maybe the last they will hear,
the tanks rolling in like a rampaging bull.
They load the gun with the missile saying,
'Fire me as fast as you can.'
Listening to a missile sounds puzzling
but the soldiers have no choice.

From this day on the war has never ended,
but we shall never know if it will go on.
No one knows when death will stop.

Tanveer Rahman (12)
The Compton School, London

War On WWII

I sit on my bed, thinking of my family, hoping I don't die.
Listening to the guns rattling like a snake.
I just want to spread my wings and fly home.
Bombs *bang,* bloody bodies
I am mentally dead, if not physically.

I hear the guns groaning, crying like a baby from shooting
I see people looting. Looting people from their lives
My best mate here is my chattering rifle
We're like ants hundreds of us crawling for our lives
I am mentally dead, if not physically.

I'm hiding in a trench, too scared to move
I hear planes overhead
In war it's a fight for the fittest, so there's nothing to prove
I wish I was in a room sleeping tight in bed
I am mentally dead, if not physically.

We hear our guns talking to us like a friend
War is for kings who want more power
A proper life we might not have ever again
War is certainly not pretty like a blooming flower.
I am mentally dead, if not physically.

Guns and knives cause death
People lie bloody and dead
People on the floor struggling for breath
Some people are lying wounded in bed
I am mentally dead, if not physically.

Nirav Vyas (13)
The Compton School, London

Deathly Silence

The silence echoes down the hall,
A reminder of the fatal fall.
The truth may linger in their thoughts,
Why did she lose the fight she fought?
She screamed for help so loud and clear,
No one heard, no one was near.
She is gone, the house is empty,
As for silence, there is plenty.

Everyone thought she was alright
But no one heard her cry all night.
He killed her there and now she's dead,
Now it's him who cries instead.
Lonely nights where silence lingers,
He feels the coldness of her fingers.
She is gone, the house is empty,
As for silence, there is plenty.

Without a word her fate was sealed,
Now she lies buried in a field.
The night she died her screams weren't heard,
What was her final whispered word?
The silence pounds loud in their ears
As they slowly drown in their own tears.
She is gone, the house is empty,
As for silence, there is plenty.

The silence may seem deathly now,
How did she die? We don't know how,
All we know, the fatal fall,
Makes silence echo through the hall.
She is gone, the house is empty,
As for silence, there is plenty.

Rebecca Hansell (13)
The Emmbrook Secondary School, Wokingham

Untitled

I sit alone, on my bed,
Knees curled up right to my head.
Weeping eyes just like a willow,
I rest my head upon my pillow.

I hear Daddy's car pull up in the drive,
I sit up tall and dry my eyes.
I wait for Daddy to come in my room,
I hear his boots go *boom, boom, boom.*

I hear the clinking of his belt,
I shiver at the thought of blows he's dealt.
My door swings open with a creak,
No noise to he heard, not a mouse's squeak.

With the belt in his hand; he drags me off the bed,
Where will he hit me this time; last night it was my head.
With his firm hand, he shoves me to the floor,
He raises the belt, he hits me more.

With my mum in the house, I dare not scream
I just wish this is a painful dream,
I hope my mummy didn't see,
That tonight my daddy murdered me.

Vicky Hellewell (13)
The Emmbrook Secondary School, Wokingham

I Took Flight

This morning I walked along a bridge,
And a bird called down to me,
'You are earthbound and I am free!
Is that why you are sad?'

'It was,' I replied now grinning, 'but now not!'
'You don't know what it's like not to be able to fly,
And therefore can't enjoy it as much as me.'
'You can't enjoy it at all!' it sneered
'Alas, I long to fly and have the willpower of
a thousand lightning bolts and can fly if I
wish it!'

And then it happened,
I could no longer feel my weight,
My legs lifted from the ground,
I was among the clouds,
Staring at the bird,
Triumphant, joyful and full of sensation.

But then it stopped,
I fell, plummeting towards the ground,
I landed with a thud, shocked and shaken,
And then continued my journey to work.

At work, after I had told my boss what happened,
He sighed and said, 'John, I've told you before,
You will never fly. It just won't happen.
It's a dream that won't come true.'

Sam Keen (11)
Trevor Roberts School, London

Free

I sat alone in a
Wide room,
The walls were
Dark and showed
The marks of many
A hungry man.

I picked up the
Gun and held it
To the target.
As I did so, here
Entered the man.

Sgt Johnson, who had
Painted my life
A shade of darkness,
He said,

'You're free, free to
Roam the world
Again, free to
Love your wife.'

I ran outside
Into that world
Of freedom, and as
I did so

The bullet hit the target.

Sam Spike (11)
Trevor Roberts School, London

Air, Fire And Earth

Air

Outside the rain falls,
In thick, driving sheets,
Against the pane.
The souls of the wind whoop,
And scream as they come past
In the night and the bare tendrils of creepers
Beat on the glass, beckoning me out into the storm.
On the sill, a single beacon of light,
From an oil lamp peers out into the darkness,
Its glow stopped short by the fog.

Fire

The light dances around the cave walls,
Amongst the ochre and clay drawings,
Breathing life into the long dead.
As the fire burns, the dance of the
Stickmen becomes frenzied,
They hunt the creatures surrounding them,
And live out their shadowy lives,
But as the veil is drawn over night,
And the fire burns low,
The figures slow and wane,
And with the arrival of the dawn,
They turn once more to dust.

Earth

Beneath the lighted moon and darkened sun,
The silent trees stand, anchored to the earth,
By their roots, which, like serpents, twist and turn,
Slipping away from the encroaching dawn.
And, in the soil, the newborn saplings reach
For the rejuvenated world above,
For the newly drained day in the world above,
Bursting from the earth at dawn's newly broken brake.

James White (15)
Wellington College, Crowthorne

More Than A King

(The poem is about my cat, Caesar)

Caesar, you were king
And the cutest little thing
You used to fight the other cats
But they were only little brats.

Your warm and cuddly fur
Almost made me purr
When I touched you with my hand
You felt like a brass-band!

Then we had to give you away
And it didn't feel okay
They were nice people though
Who let you play in the snow.

One day a high-speed car came along
And the angels sang a sad song
To us you were more than a king
We loved you more than anything!

Kasper Nikolai Ryste (11)
Willington School, Wimbledon

Healing Old Wounds

Your stench lingers
Even after you've gone
Memories embedded in my mind
Even after so long.

I can't seem to forget
After so many years
The pain you caused me
The never-ending tears.

I asked myself countless times
Why this happened to me
Screaming unanswered questions
Into darkness trying to consume me.

Some things I'll never comprehend
So I'll set myself free
From the hate, anger and deceit
Eating through me.

Afia Ameyaw-Gyarko (16)
Woodlands School, Basildon

Young Writers Information

We hope you have enjoyed reading this book - and that you will continue to enjoy it in the coming years.

If you like reading and writing poetry drop us a line, or give us a call, and we'll send you a free information pack.

Alternatively if you would like to order further copies of this book or any of our other titles, then please give us a call or log onto our website at www.youngwriters.co.uk

Young Writers Information
Remus House
Coltsfoot Drive
Peterborough
PE2 9JX

(01733) 890066